'A Diary of us Country Publicans'

The other side of Pub life.

Patrick H Bowles.

Copyright © Patrick H Bowles 2012

First printed 2012

All rights reserved.

The right of Patrick H Bowles to be identified as the author of this work has been asserted in accordance with sections 77 and 78 of the Copyright, Designs and Patents Act 1988.

INTRODUCTION

Fifteen years of enduring blood, sweat and tears in the construction industry had passed since embarking upon my adult career. Years of my life I look back on with a bizarre affection, fondness and respect, reflecting upon the trials and tribulations of the industry. One that is unique, providing on the one hand challenging opportunities, and on the other, a sense of in-describable achievement on completion of a difficult project.

Many a time have I experienced the pleasure and pride of handing keys of new dwellings to their new owners. My epitaph remains in what I have built over the years. I was leaving all this behind for a new life.

31st. December, 1987 was a memorable date for me. I had successfully managed to agree favourable terms and conditions with my then business partner to sell-out my 50% shareholding in the building business we had founded, some seven and a half years earlier. Good fortune and lady luck had been kind to us, although many a risk were taken in the quest for business, recognition and repute. We were fortunate to have been highly successful, building both profit and reputation through hard work, dedication and implicit trust in each others abilities. I am proud to reflect on the past and the achievements that both partners, subsequently directors, attained. Even after painlessly separating, we continue to remain friends to this day.

With the prospect of a new career opportunity, I decided upon my long time desire to share with my wife the prospect of being 'mine host', as the proprietors and licensees of The Dew Drop Inn, a rural 'olde-worlde' pub and restaurant establishment we knew of and intended to purchase in the heart of the Kent countryside.

The licensed trade is not an easy career. As a customer it is all to easy to be misled in thinking it is a profession full of glamour and high reward with minimum effort seen from the customer side of the bar. On the contrary, it is unbelievably hard work, requiring dedication and total commitment from everyone concerned with the venture. Any weakness or lack of commitment can only result in failure and in the worst case financial ruin.

Conversely, a successful and well run business can be a highly self-gratifying and rewarding experience. Our life experiences in the venture combined the serious with the trivial, the frustrating with the gratifying and the tedious with the downright comical.

The intention of this book is to record some of our personal experiences in the initial year we owned The Dew Drop Inn. The accounts and events are all true and factual. The characters and names are as I recollect. I apologise unreservedly in advance to any character or person should my recollection of their details be a little at odds with reality.

DEDICATION

This book is dedicated to my dearest, long suffering wife and partner Susan, who's total and complete support throughout our marriage, has enabled us both to embark on this and several other business ventures together.
It has not always been easy and on occasion's personal sacrifices have been necessary along the way. Our health, resolve and resolute determination to succeed have been our strengths whilst maintaining a proper sense of reality have been fundamental to our success, even in the face of shared adversity.
A sense of pride and humour has always prevailed throughout, even during the darkest and toughest times.

Thank you my love.

CONTENTS

CHAPTER 1 – All Change   Page 1/.

CHAPTER 2 – Full Steam Ahead!   Page 8/.

CHAPTER 3 – Laying down the law   Page 22/.

CHAPTER 4 – Myths & Legend   Page 34/.

CHAPTER 5 – Here comes Trouble!   Page 43/.

CHAPTER 6 – Up and Running   Page 65/.

CHAPTER 7 – Reality kicks in   Page 87/.

CHAPTER 8 – On the crest of a wave   Page 95/.

CHAPTER 9 – Holding it together   Page 105/.

CHAPTER 10 – Taking a breather   Page 117/.

CHAPTER 11 – Keeping momentum going   Page 128/.

CHAPTER 12 – Heads above water   Page 137/.

CHAPTER 13 – On song again   Page 147/.

EPILOGUE   Page 173/.

CHAPTER 1 – All Change

Having sold out my shareholding in a successful construction company based in Larkfield near Maidstone, the County town of Kent, I decided, along with my good lady wife to embark on a new shared business venture within the licensed trade. True to say, like most builder boys, a considerable amount of time is spent in wheeling and dealing and socialising within local pubs and hostelries, so it is not unsurprising that the lure of the pub trade was significant when a change of lifestyle was on the cards. Some might say cutting out the middle man was a commercially prudent decision on my part. Furthermore, I come from a publican's background as grandparents, great grandparents and those before were all in the licensed trade. It seemed almost a natural progression to make.
After taking all of six months viewing prospective properties, both good and bad alike the life of 'Mine Host' was decided upon within what we felt was an idyllic rural location centred within the Canterbury, Hythe and Ashford triangle high on the North Downs in our home county of Kent. The Dew Drop Inn was originally built as three cottages in Bodsham Green, Elmsted in 1485. It subsequently became the bailiff house for the estate of Sene. It resorted back to three cottages some eighty years later after the baronial estates of Sene and Newington merged. At this point in time an alehouse licence was granted for the on-site brewing and consumption of ale for sale to residents of nearby Elmsted and surrounding areas. Woodland management and coppicing were the principle activities in the area with hops being grown in former wooded areas after clearance. The heavy clay over chalk proved ideal soil properties for hop proliferation. Ale was produced on site in the two outer cottages and available for consumption in the middle cottage for the following two hundred years.
Eventually, in 1845 the ale licence was revoked in favour of a tavern licence and the former alehouse took on a coaching house status allowing the sale of alcohol to passing trade, not that there was much as the property is well off the recognised thoroughfare routes. The Prince of Wales Inn was the first name given to the establishment. As was the case with many rural public houses, the property traded as not only local pub but shop, bank, post office and virtually became the centre of the hamlet community. In 1971 the property was sold and was no longer part of a tied estate. The new owners

embarked upon an ambitious modernisation, extension and refurbishment programme completely transforming the establishment whilst maintaining all the character and history of this fine old building. Inglenook fireplaces, exposed timber beams and character windows were preserved along with major restaurant, kitchen and entrance extensions added to the existing structure. The new owners renamed the establishment The Dew Drop Inn in recognition of the former woodcutting industry in the surrounding area. A timber batt (or batten in modern connotation) is defined as a tree trunk sawn by two handed saw, normally over a tree cutting pit, cut to a cross section of 9"x 9". Offcuts s of wood and bark would be burnt for charcoal in a burning pit. During modernisation works the old cutting and burning pits were discovered giving rise to the new name. We fell in love with The Dew Drop and its location the first time we visited the establishment and decided to buy the free house as a going concern albeit with reservations as the level of trade was so low. We knew it would be an uphill challenge but the stunning rural location sold it to both us and subsequently our two young daughters.

In accordance with normal licensed trade protocol both the good lady and myself, as joint licensees, had attended the quarterly licensing sessions in Folkestone to seek and be awarded a Protection Order seven days prior to formally taking over The Dew Drop Inn. Hence the name, the purpose of the exercise was to legally provide the existing licensees 'protection from prosecution' for the sale of alcohol and tobacco until the legal transfer of the licence that would normally take place within twenty-eight days of a change in licensee. This legal formality had been completed prior to legal completion clearing the way for the formal transfer of ownership. The official licence transfer would take place after completion of the twenty-eight day 'probationary period'.

Unseasonable, beautiful blue cloudless skies greeted us on Thursday, 21st April 1988, the date the solicitors agreed for the next phase of our lives to begin.
As is customary on such handover occasions, the likes of brewery representatives, stock takers, local police and Uncle Tom Cobbly and all visit under their various guises to eke out business opportunities, duties and good old fashioned 'nosy-parker' syndrome.

I went ahead arriving shortly after 9.30am leaving the good lady to finalise the removal procedures at our former home premises and to follow on bringing the children and leading the removal lorry and team to our new home.

By rights everything should have been as sweet as a nut. I had been at the pub for the previous two days to finalise all the finer points of the business transfer and to acquaint myself with some of the locals and regulars attending the pub and the day-to-day running of the business.

Despite my best endeavours, things didn't turn out to be so simple. I arrived at The Dew Drop Inn that morning and was greeted by our stock takers; my representative and the outgoing licensee' representative. The purpose served by these persons is to establish a fair outgoing/incoming value of beer stocks, spirits, soft drinks, food, consumables, glassware etc. etc. so that the incoming licensee pays a fair price for the stock transferred. This operation is normally concluded in 1-2 hours but is generally imperative to be completed by noon so that the new business can be seamlessly up and running for normal trading hours. Sounds great in principle but in practice on this occasion nigh on impossible!

After a concerted effort knocking at all doors and windows, none of us attendees could raise any of the occupants of the pub. The last night farewell party had apparently run well into the early hours of the morning with the outgoing licensee not getting to bed until 4.30am! Only by resorting to using the local public telephone could any sign of life be instilled in the premises. Very bleary-eyed and hung-over the existing licensees and son and daughter appeared shortly before 10.30am in a totally lethargic and an almost comatose state, apparently totally oblivious to the impending business transfer. Copious quantities of coffee and Paracetamol were urgently administered to the suffering foursome. Little effect seemed apparent until the rantings from their stock taker finally struck accord.

The professionals immediately set about their task like men possessed, knowing the implications of being late were serious to say the least.

Shortly afterwards, shock horror, her ladyship, with our two daughters turned up with the removal lorry and team in tow!

A quick visit to the flat above the pub revealed the existing licensee owners had not seriously started packing up their belongings for the move. Motivating the owners from their glorious hangovers proved to be a total nightmare. Even more concerning I was advised they were moving themselves with two family cars and a somewhat decrepit trailer that had obviously seen better days. 'Removal people were so expensive these days' were cited for the reasoning for the DIY removal service!

Returning to terra firma I was first met by the good lady and removal foreman in cheerful mood, totally oblivious to the non-performance above and the obvious legal difficulty we would shortly find ourselves in as legal completion would be impossible to be effected by noon. Needless to say the mood changed markedly when the reality of the situation became clear. Smiles and good nature rapidly switched to anger, despair and facial grimaces. For my part I returned to the earlier visited telephone box to consult with our solicitor and take advice. Under normal circumstances we would expect to experience cool and level advice from our solicitor. Once I had described the scenario and sufficient time elapsed for the implications to sink in our guy seemed to morph into a totally different animal. Gone was the quiet, unassuming, professionalism to be replaced with total disbelief, panic and incredulity. I believe my solicitor thought it was my bizarre sense of humour to re-enact an April Fool Day joke on him three weeks after the event. On instruction I returned to The Dew Drop Inn, to make the vendors aware of their breach of contract and that a damages claim was in hand for presentation to their solicitors in settlement of their failure to vacate on time.

Walking back to The Dew Drop Inn the realisation and potential consequences of the situation started to race in my mind. I was facing a nightmare scenario:-

Homeless, no business, mutiny in the removal camp, professionals at each others throats etc. etc. Could it possibly get any worse?

Something or someone appeared to have got through to the vendors. It was now shortly after 11.30am and the initial two car convoy had been loaded, the decrepit trailer was hitched up, loaded with beds and mattresses. The whole scene had suddenly become manic. Was it my solicitor who had stirred them up, their solicitor, who knows. All that was obvious was they were moving, and desperately fast at that! The cars and trailer took off at a rate of knots.

I wasn't overly concerned; they were going and that was that. In the meantime, the separate restaurant area was being progressively filled up with all forms of the vendor's belongings awaiting final transfer by the in use 'convoy' vehicles.

At mid-day on the button both stock takers presented themselves to me, armed with countless bits of paper with calculations on. Both men appeared quite good natured and in high spirits. They concluded that an agreement had been reached regarding my ingoing stock level and as is customary on these occasions presented me with the analysis and the bill covering the amount I was expected to pay. Provisionally I was anticipating paying in the order of £4500. The final figure was considerably less at £2778 plus an additional £250 for my stocktaking fee. I was happy with the result and duly wrote the necessary cheques and handed them to the respective agents. Receipts were provided and we were done. The stock takers offered their farewells and hurriedly left as they were due at another venue. By this time the removal foreman was becoming a little impatient. Stating that his gang would have to go onto a day rate charge for the delay I was struck with a flash of inspiration that I thought would resolve the situation. I considered that the stock in the pub was now mine; therefore I could use it to my own ends. Noon had come and gone, technically the premises was ours. Why not do the unthinkable? Yes I would!

I went in to confirm my actions to the remaining two vendors on site. We were going to open for business!

We duly opened up the bar, offering a limited range of goods for sale. Obviously, food was not available but I thought at least this will pass the time of day for the removal men and as it was at my expense, I felt it was commercially prudent to do so. Not a single person in the removal gang argued. Even the foreman seemed to be at ease.

It was perfect weather for the time of year. So much so that walkers, ramblers and hikers were making full use of the unseasonable weather. Ironically, now in possession of a rural 'watering hole' attractive to this hardened breed of person I soon learnt the value of having such custom.

From outside, The Dew Drop Inn bordered the local village green which in fact doubled as the pub car park. Whilst in the state of flux during handing over, and our earlier decision to open for business, there was no one more surprised, nee delighted as myself, when a band of hardy walkers presented themselves in the bar looking for sustenance as our first paying customers. They seemed oblivious to the presence of the seven man removal team. After explaining we were waiting for supplies, a feeble but truthful excuse, they all indicated they had sandwiches and it was drinks and snacks they sought providing we had no objection to them using the facilities. I suggested it was such a nice day the garden would probably be an ideal location for lunch. Another stroke of brilliance! The till started playing the tunes all landlords like and we started trading for real.

As I was instructed, I rang back our solicitor for an update, this time using our pub phone. He stated due to the exceptional circumstances he had withheld the noon completion. This made sense to me and explained the obvious manic turnaround to the vendors vacating the premises. I crossed my fingers, told a little white lie stating we were still waiting. However I agreed to ring back again at 3.00pm to advise on the moving progress. I didn't think it prudent to tell him we were trading, and not that badly either!

Half an hour later, the convoy returned with two extremely red-faced drivers less the trailer. Apparently the drivers were reckoning on a journey turnaround time of 20-30 minutes. They were moving to a house just outside Canterbury only about 6 miles away. Why was it the first trip took the best part of two hours?

Apparently, the lead car driver threw a lit cigarette butt out of the window. The second car with the mattress laden trailer was following closely behind. Somehow the smouldering cigarette butt lodged in the mattresses, fanned by the draught and ignited the trailer contents. More amusingly, the driver of the second car believe it or not was in fact a fully trained fireman! The fire was only noticed when another trailing car alerted the driver in front to the smoke by flashing his headlights and overtaking whilst wildly gesticulating to the driver. Realising the problem the fireman driver slowed but took the trailer directly to Canterbury Fire Station for extinguishing. The trailer was badly damaged and the contents virtually destroyed. Our intrepid fireman was treated to the best leg pulling Kent Fire Service could offer!

The next couple of journeys were uneventful and enough clearance progress had been made enabling our removal team to vacate the bar and get on with the job in hand. They were a very efficient and slick operation and the lorry contents were emptied remarkably quickly. Amazing what a few 'freebie' pints on a nice day can do!

As previously agreed I rang the solicitor back again shortly after 3.00pm. He advised that a conditional completion had been agreed with the other side and that we could finally start moving in. I didn't have the heart to tell him we were already there and trading. I just concluded the niceties and offered an invitation for him to visit with his wife for a 'pub warming' drink.

Our removal team left shortly afterwards and the vendors continued their removal operations into the evening. I agreed their garage contents could remain until the following day.

The conditional completion was concluded with the money transferred during banking hours on the following day.

We were finally relieved as our nightmare from removal hell concluded.

The adventure had only just begun.

CHAPTER 2 – Full Steam Ahead!

Following on from the nightmare business transfer we were both keen and well fired up to make a proper start to our new livelihood. The evening session following the business transfer proved to be a disappointment and was a bit of an anti-climax.

The early trading sessions in any licensed business after a change of landlord are crucial. The new incumbent must take the opportunity to consolidate existing customers and welcome any potential newcomers. There is however a risk that former 'bad' customer's may take the opportunity to pose as new customers. Re-introducing themselves would normally be highlighted and unwelcome by the regular customers. None the less, the new owners would have to quickly try to disseminate the good from the bad. Metaphorically speaking, it was like walking a tightrope over a river with man eating sharks on one side and piranhas on the other. 'Bad boy' lists are rarely passed on from previous landlords for fear of reprisal or retribution. Such was the case in hand with our transfer. It would be left to us to make our own judgement on the visiting clientele regardless whether good, bad or existing.

As is customary throughout the trade, customers who make the effort to patronise a new owner's establishment could normally expect to be treated to the first drink on the house. In return the new landlords could expect to not only put a name to a face but be given some sort of insight to the previous owners and their running of the establishment.

Customers that night were very thin on the ground. The bar had opened at 7.00pm. The first and only customers turned up at 10.15pm. They were a young couple of love-birds out to find our remote pub for the first time on the recommendation of friends. Unaware of the recent change of ownership the initial 'freebie' went down very well. The ambience was ideal. Log fire in the inglenook burning brightly, Hulio Inglesias serenading over the background music, subdued bar lighting in the olde worlde surroundings. What more could they wish for? They stayed for a couple of drinks before moving on stating it was getting late. I believe an ulterior motive was probably in mind and bade them farewell. I shut up shop shortly after the couple left and cashed up.

Thus concluded our first night session as publicans! It was early days and we both hoped better things were to come.

Being a little cynical we both hoped the first proper trading experience was the exception rather than the rule.

Our second day proved to be far more interesting. Between us we decided the pub should initially trade 7 days a week with both lunchtime and evening sessions. We would open the lunchtime session at 12.00 noon, closing at 2.30pm and re-opening at 7.00pm for the evening session. Licensing laws at the time meant closing at 11.00pm and 10.30pm on Sundays. We had the benefit of a 'supper hour extension' for our restaurant, allowing us to legally extend the drinking session by 1 hour at the licensee' discretion if we so desired. Our view was to make our money during normal hours without having to resort to late night drinking. Apparently the previous owners were dependant upon 'late ones' to make ends meet and bolster their meagre turnover. Needless to say it was not something the previous owners were totally open about nor were we made aware of prior to making the business purchase! As we subsequently found out many of the regular customers had considered The Dew Drop Inn to be a sound bet for an illegal late, after hour's drinking session.

The brilliant sunshine from the previous day had given way to cold, low cloud and steady rainfall, dank and miserable to say the least. The fire in the bar inglenook crackled away giving a cosy warmth that could be felt in all corners of the bar. The pub that lunchtime session was as inviting as in the previous evening.

Tom Rose was the first 'local regular' customer to visit the establishment that Friday lunchtime. The weather turning inclement had meant a premature termination of the works in hand at the site Tom was working at. A life long resident in the hamlet, and the eldest of five siblings Tom lived immediately across the village green and was a true country character. In his early sixties, Tom had worked in a variety of jobs on the local farms and more recently was operating machinery for a local plant hire firm. A true country boy at heart Tom was friendly and very much at home in the Dew Drop Inn. He was one of the oldest customers that frequented the pub and by virtue of the quantity of English Ale he consumed was probably one of the best. Another of his passions was his pipe-smoking habit. Hearts of Oak tobacco was his favoured choice which gave a cherry aromatic smoke that even the most ardent non-smoker found it hard to dislike.

Characteristically, Tom was the model country bumpkin. Being quite tall, Tom would be seen wearing tweed jacket, corduroy trousers, brogues and a matching tweed trilby hat most of the time. He was most adept at telling tales about the countryside. He had one permanently straightened index finger as a result of an accidental encounter with a threshing machine. An encounter he lost but earned a permanent reminder of the accident in the process. His stubby little pewter tankard held pride of place in the overhead glass rack. When a refill was required the straight finger would normally be tapped on the rim of the tankard or counter edge, accompanied by a gruff 'When you're ready boy!' request for a refill. His place was unofficially reserved at the end of the upper saloon bar. Tom probably knew more about The Dew Drop Inn than anyone else. He didn't suffer fools gladly nor tolerate bullshit. He spoke his mind particularly on country matters and vintage motorcycle racing of which he was very fond off. He proudly boasted that he had been a drinker in the pub from the age of 14. He knew the pub pre-Dew Drop Inn renaming and could recount the past landlords, good and bad over the past 40 years or more. Tom was the machine driver who discovered the timber cutting and burning pits during the modernisation and extension works. We took an instant liking to Tom and his wife Helen even though it was quite rare to see Helen in the pub.
After exchanging the niceties of introduction Tom duly accepted my offer of an English Ale on the house. It had the desired effect. Having part poured the bottle of beer into his pewter pot; Tom pulled out his tobacco pouch, deftly lifted the pouch lid rummaged within and withdrew his filled pipe, drew on the stem and lit up the pipe with a match on the bar. He drew deeply, exhaled allowing the aromatic cloud of smoke to swirl in his immediate vicinity.
'Bit of a pipe man, eh Tom?' I passed comment 'Used to be one myself in earlier times.' I continued.
Tom just grunted and nodded, enjoying the pipe smoke. He was having his own little solitary moment, only stopping to have another slurp of his beer.
'So what brings you here then boy?' he asked.
'Oh it's such a lovely pub, so rural and quiet.' I replied.
'You've got yer work cut-out 'ere boy. Old Geoff really struggled.' Tom counter replied

'Funny pub, funny buggers get in 'ere too' he continued. 'Still you've got to take it to survive boy.' Tom drew on his pipe again, emptied the bottle of beer into his pot, raised it to his mouth and emptied the contents.

Placing the pewter pot back on the counter I had my first experience of the re-ordering finger process accompanied by 'When you're ready boy!' request for a refill.

I duly obliged by placing another English Ale on the bar after removing the top.

'How much do you want?' Tom asked

'That's a pound mate.' I replied.

'Bugger me! That doesn't happen often. Old Geoff was charging five pence more the old rogue!' whilst sliding a pound coin over the bar. My predecessor obviously considered Tom a soft touch. The stock taker had advised the new price charged which I was happy with.

'There you go Tom, lower price more beer. VFM that's what we offer' I retorted.

'What the bloody hell's VFM?' Tom asked.

'Value for money mate' I replied jokingly.

'I think we're going to get on fine!' the older man responded, drew on his pipe and took another swig of his beer.

The latch of the door lifted and the door opened. My second customer of the day walked in to the bar.

A short, wiry-haired and wrinkled little man came to the bar. Seeing Tom sitting on his 'perch' he acknowledged his presence, turned to me enquiring if I was the new landlord. I answered in the affirmative asking if I could get him something.

'Derek Leach' he answered 'Landlord of the Bull Inn in Hastingleigh' he continued. The Bull Inn was in fact the nearest pub competition to us, about 3 miles away.

'Pat Bowles of The Dew Drop Inn' I replied, whilst offering a friendly handshake.

'What can I get you?' I offered.

'Thanks. Just a half of bitter' Derek replied

I pulled the beer and placed it on the bar in front of him. Derek went for his money to pay. 'No mate, that's with me.' I assured him.

'Thanks very much.' He replied lifting the glass to drink.

Only then did he address Tom. 'So how's things Tom?'

'Not so bad Dell' Tom replied almost without interest drawing on his pipe again.

"'ere Dell; our old mate here is charging a quid for his English Ale. How come you're charging £1.10?' Tom went straight on the offensive.

Derek's eyes were everywhere, gleaning every little piece of detail of the pub he could. He was obviously caught on the hop and was very uneasy at Tom's challenge and tried to ignore the comment. Re-addressing me he went on with the normal courtesies and niceties extended to opposing visiting landlords.

'Got any serious plans Pat?' he enquired

'It's too early to say at the moment.' I answered 'Real ale. Bit of bar food, that sort of stuff' I continued

'Best ham, egg and chips in the area we do!' Derek boasted.

'I must make a point of trying it sometime.' I responded courteously, not really ever intending to do so.

Derek rapidly emptied the half pint glass, set it on the bar, offered his thanks, bade his farewell and left.

'Watch 'im. He's a Nasty bastard!' Tom muttered. 'He'll stir the shit for you. Guarantee it!' From the manner of Tom's mutterings I concluded Derek, and his establishment were not one of Tom's favourite.

'When you're ready boy!' Tom requested another beer and re-stoked his pipe.

Much at the same time the new landlady made her entrance behind the bar. Coinciding with Tom's earlier request I passed the opened beer bottle to Tom and formally made the introduction. At the same time the bar door opened and another couple entered the bar. Clearly they were locals and knew Tom.

Christina was the baby of the Rose clan; Tom's youngest sister who was accompanied by husband Jack, Tom's brother-in-law. They too lived across the green, next door to Tom and Helen and shared their house with Mrs Rose, the most senior surviving member of the Rose clan. Mrs Rose was following on later.

Introduction formalities concluded and gratefully received free drinks poured; the mood lightened and became a little less formal and more relaxed. The landlord and landlady were keen to make a good impression as 'mine hosts' but not overly so, whilst maintaining an element of decorum. Mrs Rose joined the party shortly afterwards.

She was a very mature lady, both worldly and wise in the ways and customs of countryside life and highly respected in the hamlet as a result. She was keen not to miss out on meeting and vetting the latest pub landlords. She had resided in the hamlet all her life and was the oldest resident. She too had seen countless owners of the pub come and go.

So far so good, the new publicans seemed to be acceptable to the customers of the pub. Word was obviously spreading via the country 'jungle telegraph' that The Dew Drop Inn was under new ownership. The bar was filling up with other patrons nicely. The village green car park was likewise filling up, always a good sign of a good hostelry.

Susan the landlady busied herself outback in the kitchen, hurriedly preparing a range of snacks that could be made available for sale to the now filling up bar. Food stocks comprised of the 'inherited' stock which was somewhat limited to frozen products that only needed deep frying for preparation. It wasn't ideal, but needs must until a new menu was created and restocking could be undertaken. Heavily salted chips and onion rings were put on the bar to entice customers. The heavy salting hopefully generated a thirst leading to more beverage sales. It was also a means to reduce the old stocks in the freezers. As it was another 'freebie' it was going down rather well and wet sales were responding accordingly.

Tom for his part was clearly in for the session. The lower priced English Ale played a major part in his thinking, coupled with the ability to vet customers as they arrived. Any 'dubious' or undesirables were quickly made known to mine host which I was very grateful for the insight. Additional freebie English Ales for Tom were made available as reward for the information. It was also clearly fortuitous to me in building a new friendship bond, cheap at half the price I concluded.

By the time 'time' was called for the close of the lunchtime session Bob, Tom's immediate younger brother had been into investigate the new owners. Bob was our direct neighbour to the rear of the pub. He lived in a tied bungalow to the farm that surrounded the pub with his wife Sal. Bob was the Little Holt Farm shepherd and fix-it man. The farm was a combination of arable and livestock so Bob was split between tractor work, stockman and shepherd. Bob was another true country character but a quieter, solitary man, less flamboyant in character to his elder brother. Bob was a cold Guinness man but only stopped for a couple of swift halves as work commitments were pressing. The opportunity to vet the new incomers couldn't be missed though.

Bob would undoubtedly inform his boss, the farmer Jim Peterson of his findings regarding the suitability of the new licensees.

The session finished on an encouraging note. Our personalities initially seemed to fit in with the locals.

Conveniently we had an afternoon visit from Stan our soft drinks rounds man who was worth his weight in gold. He had supplied the previous owners throughout their occupation and so had a good insight into the level of trade at any particular time and could advise accordingly. Our stocks of juices, soft drinks and mixers were replenished that afternoon. Similarly, the Phoenix brewery sales representative had likewise called in between sessions to meet us and pitch for our business. It certainly was not the best offer we had received for our beer and cider supply so much to his disappointment we only agreed an interim limited supply arrangement, pending a pencil sharpening exercise to increase our discount standing. He did at least leave with an initial order for beer supplies to be delivered the following Monday. It was a great disappointment to him that the lucrative spirit order was to be placed with an alternative wholesaler whose offer was so much more favourable. Every penny counts in this trade!

The Dew Drop Inn past level of trade was obviously low in comparison to other like-for-like establishments in the vicinity. Not that there were many competitors, the very rural setting of the pub with the hamlet population of only 24 meant business generation was very dependent upon 'trip out', rather than local customers. The lunchtime session that day was encouraging but nowhere near what would be required to survive. Businesses in such rural positions have to arguably try harder and offer more to entice the punters. The ever present threat of Drink-Drive laws would clearly need to be carefully considered as to the impact on the pub business. Sure the premises was so remote one rarely encountered the 'Boys in Blue'. It would be far more common to meet escaping livestock on the lanes than our law enforcement colleagues.

On the other side of the coin was the sinister argument. Being so rural and away from civilisation meant the minimum of intervention from the law and licensing authorities. Irresponsible customers would undoubtedly ignore running the risk of being caught 'over the top' by using un-patrolled rural lanes to drive home regardless of their alcohol consumption or drunken state.

Not that we intended to fall foul of the law we received our first head on encounter with the reality of 'late one' culture at The Dew Drop Inn during the very first proper evening session of our ownership. Right on the stroke of 7.00pm we opened the doors for the evening session. Completely to our pleasant surprise the car park was over half full with parked vehicles. No sooner than I had time to stoke the fire, put an extra log on and get behind the bar the bar door opened and a lot of boisterous youngsters entered the saloon bar. In no time at all the immediate bar space was filled with the newcomers, who I gathered were students from the local agricultural college in Wye, some 6 miles away. The jubilant mood they were in spoke for itself. The pub had really come to life. In the melee that followed I gave up trying to remember faces and names. The first free drinks were going down well. Lager and bitter were the preferred choice. It was extremely difficult to keep track of who had what. Invariably some 'chancers' pushed their luck and tried to claim a second 'freebie'. The resulting refusal meant the busy spell became somewhat short-lived. Clearly the student intention was to have a free drink at our expenses as a novelty and return to the heavily subsidised Student Bar back in Wye. It was the first of many frustrating occasions we would have to endure during our ownership of the pub. With the exception of four students who, unbeknown to me were residents of the Bodsham hamlet, the bar sadly quickly emptied. My only hope was that perhaps they may return and see fit to be paying customers next time.

The remaining students, two boys and two girls, introduced themselves, explaining they were living in the rented hall of residence a short distance up the road, offered apologies for their colleagues' poor behaviour, and bought a round of drinks and settled in for the evening. They struck me as very pleasant and totally different from the earlier 'rabble'. They were in their final year of study and were good customers until leaving the college later in the year.

The rain was still teeming down, driven by an ever increasing wind. It really was miserable outside. Tom returned with Helen once the bulk of the student exodus was over. He was not overly keen on the student fraternity from Wye.

'Bloody hooray 'enries who think farming's a big pissup, boy!' was his first comment, prior to introducing Helen. I had pre-empted his arrival by having an English Ale and his pot ready for him on the bar top. Tom was suitably impressed and settled on to his stool with Helen alongside. Helen was a quiet, petite woman, not the type of person you would have thought would have been Tom's stable mate. She was a sherry drinker and was most grateful for the first drink on the house, particularly as I made it a schooner, the equivalent of a double! I had already decided this couple would be valuable friends in the area.

Business remained brisk throughout the evening. It was a Friday night and many of the farm workers took the opportunity to relax and take their partners out for the evening.

Being the new kids on the block was an added attraction as the free initial drink was also an enticement.

Terry and Molly Pay was one such couple. They lived in the end of terrace house across the village green with their two young children. Their children were much the same age as our two. The four children were destined to become good friends as they were in the same class at school. Terry worked for a local agricultural contractor as a tractor driver for his living; long and unsociable hours, and earning a small basic wage to boot. Excessive working hours were a necessity to make ends meet. Molly did a little part-time work cleaning at the big house of the village. Molly was to play a significant role in the pub operation in due course when new staff members were being recruited. The couple received their initial free drink with thanks and entered into conversation with Tom and Helen.

Jack, Christina and Mrs. Rose came across to the pub again. They were regular Friday night patrons.

The whole atmosphere was very pleasant. It was becoming clearly obvious that the pub really was the centre of the micro community. Everyone seemed to know everyone else including their business, circumstances etc., etc. They were joined by Bob and his wife Sal shortly afterwards.

Time was marching on. It was about 9.30pm and the comings and goings continued. Some customers stayed longer than others.

Thankfully no one was looking for food as we both realised we were woefully ill prepared or stocked for what we wanted to offer on our new menu.

Crisps, snack biscuits and nuts were the main requests, for which we had plenty of stock.

Other customers kept appearing from the surrounding area and outlying villages. The surprising common factor was that everyone seemed to know each other quite well, regardless where they came from. The evening was moving along nicely and the friendly atmosphere was growing as time passed by. The business takings were finally showing some sort of credence even after taking in to account the introductory free drink. The car park was full and parking was over spilling onto the narrow lanes at the front and side of the pub. Both of us were busy behind the bar with little time to indulge in conversation. This, I concluded to myself, is what the business should be doing.

As I turned back to the bar I couldn't help but notice four faces that were very familiar to me.

'Found you, you old bugger!' the leading man exclaimed. It was Neil a former employee of mine along with three other former workmates, Chris, Peter and Grant. Six months earlier the four guys were working for me on the site of a new drug rehabilitation centre that I was overseeing. We had become good friends and drinking partners at the same time. The foursome had taken it upon themselves to track us down to our new abode. It was great to see them and four freebie pints were duly served to them. Even my wife was touched at seeing them. She knew them well by way of contact through the business and as barmaid at our local pub where she was gaining trade experience before taking on The Dew Drop Inn.

More and more new faces appeared, few seemed to be leaving. In desperate vain I was finding it increasingly difficult to keep track and remember names and faces. Sue was similarly affected. I for my part resorted to using 'mate' as standard addressing; Sue resorted to 'Luv or My Luv'. It seemed to be universally accepted by all.

By now it was nearing 10.30 pm and still the customers were coming. Rod Rose, the youngest son of the family called in accompanied by Terry Burk, alias 'Smurve' as known by the locals. The two men had been at work elsewhere and finished a late shift, deciding to pop in and greet us newcomers. Rod, like his brothers primarily worked on the farm, turning his hand to any skill needed at the time. The quest for more money however made Rod the 'maverick' of the family.

He would change occupation readily if a quick buck could be made. Smurve was a sub-contract glazier by trade, working wherever employment was available regardless of what was on offer. Both Rod and Smurve were friends as a result of working together when chasing the right employment opportunity. On this occasion they were working together on a new-build shopping complex in Folkestone. It had been a physically hard day for both of them in the concreting gang. Rest and relaxation was the name of the game which naturally meant a lot of 'thirst quenching' in the process.

In no time at all the new arrivals had somehow met up with my former employees and were soon swapping building tales and experiences together. It really was so friendly.

Another late arrival, Jake and Emma joined the throng in the pub. Jake was a lorry driver on a local circuit collecting and delivering eggs from one of the local battery production farm units. He was in his final year of working pending retirement. His partner Emma, affectionately known as 'Evil Emma' was one of the local gossips. What Emma didn't know about the local scene or local telegraph wasn't worth knowing! She had already retired some years before enabling her to keep permanently up-to-date with local events and happenings.

The party-like atmosphere kept building as did the temperature in the bar area. There was an immediate knock-on effect to the sales of drinks. On one of the rare moments I had to exchange niceties with Tom, he informed me he couldn't recall seeing the pub so busy or apparent sales so high. His personal effort spoke for itself. He had consumed over two thirds of a crate of English Ale single-handed! It was music to my ears, but exhausting at the same time!

At 10.50 pm, ten minutes late, the good lady rang last orders on the bar bell sited immediately adjacent to Tom's 'perch', indicating the start of the customary twenty minute drinking up time. It is always an important time in the trade. Normally, the ringing would instigate a final flurry of business before the final closure of the bar.

Syd & Pauline appeared in the bar alongside Tom and Helen introducing themselves directly to both of us behind the bar. Syd was a good friend of Tom's.

Syd worked as a self-employed welder and metalworker and was a master of his trade. He knew Tom from work as he had often been called to carry out running repairs to site machinery that Tom was operating.

'When your ready boy?' accompanied by Tom's distinctive tap on the pewter pot rang through 'And whatever Syd and Pauline are 'aving.' Tom ordered.

Helen engaged in conversation with Pauline leaving the two men recounting earlier exploits. I duly served them and then made an effort to clear the bar of empty glasses in what I thought would be preparation for the imminent bar closure, or so I thought!

The party atmosphere was in still full swing with everyone enjoying themselves. The good lady and I were both exhausted albeit happy that the show was on the road in such a decisive manner. Not being 'acclimatised' to our new roles in life, we were both almost ready for our beds. There was however the matter of clearing up, glass washing, re-stocking, cashing up and bedding down the fire before we could consider retiring, let alone the minor problem of having approximately sixty customers still in the bar!

'Final bell' went through my mind quickly. By now it was 11.10pm. I went for the bell on the wall by Tom and Syd, still deeply engrossed in conversation.

'Wait a minute!' I thought to myself. The bell body and clapper were not there anymore! The brass support gallows bracket was there, but no bell. Someone had hijacked our only means of ringing time!

Syd was the first to notice my perplexed state.

'What's up mate? You lost something?' he asked in a quizzical manner. He maintained a totally straight face, Tom likewise. The two women were still deep in conversation. 'Butter wouldn't melt in their mouths – innocence personified' I thought to myself. If it wasn't them who could it be?

Smurve came to the bar requesting six pints of Fosters lager, apparently oblivious to my confused state. I just served him, ruling him out at the 'thief'.

'When your ready boy?' Tom retorted again. Syd ordered his round for the four at the bar and asked for 'one-in-the-wood' for Rod and Smurve. They knew each other well and their respective paths had crossed on building sites. Syd continued 'Pat one for Sue and yourself as well!'

I duly obliged and served accordingly.

I had to conclude to myself there was little to do but grin and bear the current situation. In compensation however we were making a good level of sales even though we were technically serving after our own targeted opening hours. As a precaution the outside lights were turned off and curtains drawn in the bar.

By 12.30am trade was beginning to fall off. With the exception of Tom and Rod the rest of the Rose clan, Helen included had retired to their beds. Jake and Emma were not serious night owls and left shortly afterwards as had the majority of the customers who were 'passing in the night'. Grant and Chris had succumbed to excess drink and exhaustion and retired to the back seat of the car to sleep. I for my part tried to socialise with Tom, Syd, Rod, Smurve and my former employees whilst Sue seemed to be getting on very well with Pauline and Molly. Terry was long gone as he had a very early start the following morning. It was a pleasant wind down to our first proper evening trading session. Secretly, we both hoped the end was not far away.

Syd suggested a final beer and short chaser to his colleagues. Tom declined as did Neil and Peter. Neil being the driver decided time to make a move. It was great and heartfelt that my former workmates came to visit. They vowed to return, hinting at some sort of reunion with other members of my construction company, bidding their farewell on leaving. Tom left with the other two and escorted Molly back home. Rod got up to leave, walking to the door, stopping and turning round announcing,

'Almost forgot! You'll probably need this then?' Rod handed back the missing brass bell in the process. 'Cheers' Rod left chuckling to himself. The bell- knapper was finally uncovered much to the mirth of the others and our embarrassment.

Syd, Pauline and Smurve finally left after Syd's second chaser. Pauline was driving and left with the two 'happy' men. Smurve left his car for collection the following day.

It never ceases to amaze be how some people can work physically hard all day, go on the 'lash' deep into the night, have minimal sleep and be up with the lark day in, day out.

The good lady wife and I were nearing total exhaustion. Our first experience in our new occupation to date had been something of a baptism by fire. It was now just after 1.35am.

Surely tonight's late episode was an exception, not the norm? Golden rules of the Trade decree various fundamental points. Customers are always right, smile even when your crying, no personal dirty washing in public, cash only as credit refusal causes offence, keep a sense of humour summarize the main points. There are countless others but they all seem to pan into oblivion when you are totally knackered, only want your bed and 'mine host' convention means being nice to people intent on 'taking the piss' to the extreme in your own home. The glamour of a publican's life may appear appealing to many. You question your sanity on such occasions that we had just experienced, rule book or not. 'Was it really worth it?' were my final thoughts as I sank into a very deep and deserved sleep.

CHAPTER 3 – Laying down the law

The events of the first Friday late night trading experience came as a bit of a shock to the new publicans. It was totally unforeseen and unwelcomed to the new owners at that time, although the additional income did prove useful. Such occasions in the future would have to be planned and somehow be controlled to be on the Landlord's terms, not on those of the customer's. Both licensees' were struggling the morning after to get the establishment up and ready for trade. It was early days and having to do everything single-handedly to meet session deadlines was proving more difficult than anticipated. Not unexpectedly, we concluded an urgent change in our life-style would be necessary to meet the commitment. Late nights would be required initially to appease the existing clientele and bolster the business. It was not however going to feature as a long term solution.

The previous owners had the benefit of extra family support in the running of the business. I had already realised we would need to recruit some help as soon as possible. The problem was being so rural. Help was not readily available to hand or so we thought?

Just prior to opening a young attractive girl presented herself at the rear kitchen door. She introduced herself as Sara, Jack and Christina's daughter from over the road. Sara was seventeen years old and in her last year at school doing her A-levels and was looking for part-time work. She had on occasions worked for our predecessors, waitressing and as a kitchen assistant handling menial tasks. She was attractive, smart and appeared very mature for her age. We both took a liking to Sara and offered her immediate part-time work on Friday nights and during the weekend sessions, primarily waitressing in the restaurant and assisting in the kitchen areas. She was delighted and after popping home to change, returned to assist Sue in the kitchen. Our previously planned limited Bar Menu was now imperative to get underway. The extra assistance Sara offered enabled the good lady to dash out to our local Cash and Carry for urgently needed supplies. Sara in the meantime busied herself with preparing some salad garnishes and generally getting ready for the lunchtime session.

At much the same time a white Astra van turned onto the car park. An elderly lady got out and hobbled round the rear of the building to the kitchen entrance.

Lorna, the local milk lady of notoriety had called to make her presence known. Lorna, a widow who was nearing seventy, not only had the milk round but jointly with her daughter and son-in-law ran a smallholding just outside the hamlet. They reared chickens, ducks, turkeys and pigs which were available fresh from the farm and oven prepared or jointed, as were free range duck and chicken eggs. They also offered a comprehensive range of vegetables throughout the year. With her regular dairy delivery round Lorna was to become a longstanding supplier to us for eggs, meat and seasonal vegetables as well as all our milk and cream requirements. Lorna called three times a week, normally late morning making The Dew Drop Inn her mid round coffee stop. She was a great character in the community covering a surprisingly large area and never too busy to stop and chat. Her round kept her in the loop of country life. Like Evil Emma, what Lorna didn't know on the 'grapevine' was not worth knowing. She was also a lifeline to a lot of the older folk. She would collect prescriptions, papers, groceries and the like and deliver to the door for those less fortunate folk she came across and at no charge. Lorna was a most kind-hearted person and received an MBE in recognition of her services to the community as a result shortly afterwards.

I had been on the go constantly getting the bar ready to open. All the domestic tasks, previously undertaken by Sue were suddenly anyone's game. Dusting, polishing, hoovering, toilet cleaning all had to be done daily along with the bar preparation, re-stocking, barrelling and the like. Fire maintenance and log re-stocking was a filthy operation, but necessary all the same. At weekends 'pipe cleaning' was an essential operation to maintain all the draught beers in pristine condition. A cellar man would normally undertake the bar duties in most pubs. Cellar men were few and far between in Bodsham so it was down to 'yours truly' to get done. I believe I was busier now than I had ever been in my lifetime. Everything had to be completed no later than 11.30am to enable a final shower and change before opening at Noon.

That day was no different to any other. I had rushed through my duties, employed Sara, met Lorna and placed orders and just managed a quick shower and change to be ready to open directly at 12.00am. As I went to unlock I was surprised to note the number of cars in the car park. Clearly, I remember Smurve's car being left but no others that I could recall.

The car park was now over half full. No sooner had I opened up a customer appeared in the bar. A new face I thought, not one I recognised from the previous evening. A somewhat red-faced short gentleman came to the bar, asking for the menu. I started to panic inwardly, made some sort of excuse and popped out to the kitchen quickly. Sara was well prepared and a little angel. Salad garnishes were neatly laid out, fryers heating up, surfaces cleared, ironmongery wrapped in napkins ready to go. She had even found time to prepare a large catering saucepan of spring vegetable soup on the stove.
'Good old Knorr soups, who would be without them!' I thought.
I quickly picked up our draft menu and returned to the bar offering it to the patiently waiting customer.
'You don't remember us, do you?' he asked. I struggled in trying to place him. 'We came up on Thursday, remember?' The penny dropped.
'Of course, you're the ramblers who stayed over for lunch!'
'Well we're back. St.George's day ramble you know. Beautiful countryside, lovely pub' he continued. 'This time a snack pub lunch is in order we thought.'
I started to panic again. I had no idea what we actually could offer and just hoped the good lady would return as soon as possible.
'What's the soup today old chap?' he asked. Without hesitance I replied 'Spring Vegetable sir'
'Mmm, it's one of my favourites! Right leave this with me.' The short man left the bar to confer with his co-ramblers, about twenty four in total. About ten minutes later he returned with an order written out on the reverse of the draft menu.
'What we would like to do is go walkies and be back for 1.30pm giving you a chance to prepare this lot. Is that alright then?'
I thanked my lucky stars. We would probably be able to meet the deadline, dependent upon the speedy return of Sue.
I looked at the order and saw 16 soup starters, 8 fish and chips, 4 cheese ploughman lunches, 5 Lincolnshire sausages and chips and 7 ham, egg and chips. My mind raced and tried to return to the stock takers list. I recalled that most of the items were listed but how much, who knows.
'That's fine sir.' I replied.
'Okay old chap see you then. Cars are okay out here eh?' the satisfied man uttered on his exit.
'Yeah, fine, see you soon'

I quickly returned to the kitchen. Sara looked at the order, counted the salad garnishes, stirred the soup and calmly appeared unflustered. I went to our freezer store room and lifted the first chest lid. Bags of chips and vegetables were present. I moved to the next freezer and lifted the lid. There were Battered fish portions by the box load. It was so far so good. Next freezer revealed sausages, great. Next freezer contained part baked rolls. Things were all okay so far. Potential problem with ham and cheese though.

In the meantime Sara had concluded we would be short on soup so a second large pot was put on to cook. Trays of the frozen food were filled up in preparation for frying.

Just at that moment along similar lines as Mafeking being relieved, Sue returned from the cash and carry trip.

I rushed out the back entrance to meet her and check on what she had purchased.

Panic over. Ham, pate, cheddar and stilton cheese, pickles were all there. Much relieved I assisted with the unloading and left the two women to continue with the food preparation.

Back in the bar, I pulled through samples of the real ales to check them for clarity and taste following the 'pipe cleaning' operation I completed earlier. It was my time to relax a little and savour the fruits of my labours. The beers couldn't have tasted better!

Smurve was the first regular customer of the day. He had walked from Smeeth where he lived to the pub where he had left his car the night before.

'Blimey, where is everyone?' he uttered on entering the bar.

'Walkers out on the hills mate' I answered. 'There back at half-one or so. Fosters?'

Smurve nodded approval and took his position at the bar.

'One for you?' he offered

'Cheers mate I'm alright at the moment' indicating the line of samples I had lined up.

'What a great night last night was eh? Those old boys who worked for you seemed alright, a great laugh.' Smurve passed comment and then drew on his beer.

' Yeah – sound bunch of lads' I replied.

''aven't seen this place that busy since old man Grattan left.'

Smurve like the others was a long time user of the pub as well and knew the previous four landlords.

The door opened and the likes of Jim Peterson and family stepped in. Smurve knew them all and acknowledged them in a friendly manner. Jim Peterson lived on and ran his Little Holt Farm with his wife. Bob was his right-hand man. Jim's daughter Ann also helped out with the book-keeping, but being a young mother and having a daughter of only eighteen months found her time stretched. Jeff her husband worked as a cabin purser for long haul British Airways and was away from home a lot. As and when Jeff was home he too would help out on the farm. Saturday and Sunday lunchtimes were regular sessions that Jim and family would normally attend. They were all very conservative AK mild drinkers and had been branded the 'AK Gang' by other regulars. Furthermore, whenever 'freebie bar food' was available the 'AK Gang' would be at the head of the queue to participate. Tom would refer to them as the 'free lunch brigade' in his own inimitable style.

Introductions completed, and 'freebie' AK mild served, the expectant new arrivals subsequently engaged in friendly banter and conversation with Smurve.

Bob and Sal shortly joined the others in the lower saloon bar area. I took the opportunity to check in the kitchen to find all was well. In fact both women had done well. Not only was the food well on its way to completion, for the first time the good lady had used the initiative to utilise the restaurant area. Sara had previous experience of the facility which was ideal for a party of twenty four as and when they arrived albeit somewhat hurriedly brought in to service.

Things were coming together so we thought. Little by little progress was being made. Both of us were flying blind and by the seat of our pants. Ones instincts were all we had to go on and just hoped we were getting it right.

12.45 right on the button and I noticed Tom's work pickup return home from his Saturday morning shift. Fifteen minutes later he was in the bar, changed from overalls, pipe spewing smoke and ready for sustenance. I duly obliged by having his beer and pot ready on the bar.

'Mornin' all!' he retorted, oblivious to the time of day, took his place at the bar, poured his beer and took a long draw from his pot. 'That's better!' Tom had landed.

Another couple of new faces entered the bar and took stools adjacent to Tom. Colin and Suzanne lived about two and a half miles away, and with the assistance of Suzanne's brother they were dog breeders and ran a kennels just between Hastingleigh and Waltham. Colin had been a successful air-conditioning engineer in London before selling out, moving to the country and changing lifestyle.

Suzanne was the true dog lover and the brains behind the business. Between them they owned and had bred twelve Newfoundland dogs of varying ages. This breed of dog has wonderful characteristics and was brought to fame in the book and Disney film, Peter Pan as Nana, the children's nurse.

After formal introduction and my insistence the first drink was on the house Colin asked for a large Famous Grouse whiskey with a lime Perrier mixer for himself and half of lager for Suzanne. The combination of scotch whiskey and lime flavoured mineral water struck me as strange, almost unpalatable. I double checked with Colin to which he re-confirmed his concoction. As time bore out, Colin used to drink this mixture in copious quantities. He particularly liked The Dew Drop Inn because the Perrier with lime twist was a stock item, rarely found in other establishments in the vicinity. I struck up quite an interesting conversation with Colin and Suzanne. I surprised them both when I correctly identified the Newfoundland breed of dog charm Suzanne was wearing on her necklace. It was a defining moment in time for me.

Business remained brisk as our intrepid St. George's Day ramblers returned. On entering the bar the pained expressions were obvious as there was little in the way of free seating. I quickly gained the attention of their leader I had dealt with earlier and made him aware of the arrangements made for his party in the adjoining restaurant area. He was obliged and duly set about ushering his party next door, but only after they had made their initial drinks purchase. It was almost military precision which caused an inner wry smile to me. The busy little man's similarity to Captain Mannering in Dad's Army struck me as striking. I had to struggle to control my mirth. Tom, not the most diplomatic person in the world had spotted my mirth.

'What's so bloody funny?' he blurted out loud.

'Nothing mate, private joke' I replied. That was clearly not going to pacify Tom. Luckily, enough time had elapsed and 'Captain Mannering' had moved on through.

By this time both Colin and Suzanne was intent on hearing some sort of explanation as well.

I lowered my voice and gave my explanation.

'The guy just gone in the restaurant, who does he remind you of?'
All three looked vacantly at me. Colin emptied his glass, Tom drew on his pipe and Suzanne expression was somewhat pained.
'Who?' Tom answered for all three.
'It's Captain Mannering from Dad's Army!' I struggled to keep my composure.
A short pregnant pause followed after which all three burst into spontaneous raucous laughter.
The session continued in good spirit and the level of business was most encouraging. The kitchen was coping well with orders for food that were picking up as customers became more aware of the extra service on offer. It was an encouraging start to the catering side of the operation.
Additional customers came and went on a steady flow throughout the session. The 'AK Gang' members were the first of the regular customers to leave. They seemed happy enough saying they would return the following day.
Colin ordered ham sandwiches for himself and his partner with a bowl of chips to share in addition. He also recharged the glasses for both Suzanne and Tom alike offering me a drink in the process. I declined gracefully, indicating the row of 'tasters' yet to be consumed.
Tom obliged me by putting an extra log on the fire. The apple log quickly started to burn. The hypnotic flames were soon dancing in the grate and were a picture to watch. Many a time passed by in quieter spells when I became mesmerised by the flaming spectacle. There is undoubtedly a mystical charm surrounding an open log fire.
Shortly afterwards, the rambling party made their way back into the bar, led by the Captain Mannering look-alike. Each male person in turn approached the bar and paid their dues for the meal they had just consumed. Everyone was most complimentary. 'Captain Mannering' was the last to settle up. He paid his dues, thanked me for our efforts, stated they would be back and with military precision led the way out of the pub with his party in tow. My earlier observation touched an accord with the upper saloon bar trio, who just burst into laughter again. I could do little but to join them.
Sara appeared from the kitchen with Colin and Suzanne's sandwiches and chips and enquired if we were alright. I assured her we were and she returned to the kitchen totally confused to relay her encounter to Sue.

Sue appeared behind the bar, enabling me to make the introduction to Colin and Suzanne. With the formalities over she left after making it clear the kitchen was now closed. This was a mutually agreed decision to stop serving food from the kitchen at 2.00pm enabling time for clearing up before pub closing. On this occasion it had been a resounding success. Both women had performed extremely well. Long may it continue!

With every modern catering kitchen appliance to their disposal, the clearing up operation did not take that long. The kitchen staff members appeared in the bar for a well deserved relaxing drink. Sara had a large orange juice and lemonade, Sue opted for a glass of lemonade. They both earned their drink rewards. A fitting end to what had been a good trading lunchtime session.

Surprisingly enough, the bar emptied reasonably quickly. Tom and Smurve left together, shortly followed by Sara leaving us four in the bar. Sara had confirmed she would be back at 6.30pm for the evening session.

Colin asked if a final round was in order as the time had gone beyond 2.30pm. I agreed as the late round was on my terms. Having served the drinks Suzanne reverted back to our earlier conversation regarding Newfoundland dogs.

Sue a long time dog lover quickly became involved in our discussion. Suzanne was emphatic that the Newfoundland breed was a master in its class. Its popularity was however waning as the breed of dog was not cheap to keep. Colin sat on the sidelines sipping at his concoction.

Suzanne must have sensed both of our interest in learning about this special breed of dog. We had never had a dog in our married life before. Geoff the previous owner owned a Doberman. Being so rural, a dog would invariably take the place of a burglar alarm. Chances are that any response to an alarm call would take at least an hour before anyone turned up. A canine deterrent or two would probably provide peace of mind. However, even though we were considering a 'guard dog' we had the two children to consider. Perhaps the solution was staring us in the face.

Newfoundland dogs were fantastic with children on the one hand; on the other hand, their sheer size would be extremely intimidating to any potential burglar.

Colin intervened. 'Why not come up to the kennels and meet Ben, Mojo and the others?'

It was an invitation Sue would never refuse, on the contrary, she decided there and then to take up Colin's offer.
The three of them left the pub shortly afterwards. Sue would be initiated to the Newfoundland breed.
Sue returned by 4.30pm, totally indoctrinated by Colin and Suzanne and their insight to Newfoundland dogs. Ben was the alpha male. He was magnificent. He was getting on in years and was Suzanne's pride and joy. In his earlier years he had been a Crufts supreme champion of breed. Even in his dotage years he would lay majestically at the kennel entrance gate looking as good as any lion in Trafalgar Square. Mojo was one of Ben's great grandchildren. She was a fine example of breed and had recently delivered four puppies. Newfoundland bitches do not make good mothers. There sheer size, in relation to the size of their offspring put the pups at risk from the moment of birth. Suzanne was an experienced breeder and was aware of all these potential problems. She had hand-reared countless puppies in the past. Newfoundland puppies are therefore in very high demand. The supply is extremely restricted hence the breed is rarely that popular. The cost of owning such an animal is also very high. The breed not only costs a lot in food, they require more than average input from the vet. Their sheer size makes them very prone to mishap and associated problems.
Sue had taken everything on board and basically decided at some point a Newfoundland dog should become a family pet. I was happy to go with the flow on the matter. There would be no doubt how our daughters would feel about the matter as and when the time came!
Whilst my good lady was away at Colin and Suzanne's kennels I shut up shop. By instinct I felt we must have done quite well and cashed up the takings. Clearly the rambling party provided a major boost to the business and could not be counted on as a regular occurrence.
However, the final total was most encouraging and on checking was well above our targeted taking for a Saturday lunchtime session. I was delighted.
Buoyed up by the earlier takings revelation I went about re-setting the bar for the evening session. Having completed the task I turned my attention to the restaurant. The small bar had been unused for sometime. A total rethink would be required before bringing it in to service. The table layout was totally impractical and illogical.
The second toilet facility was similarly unused, why I was not sure.

The inglenook fireplace was back to back with it's bar counterpart and sported the most amazing cast iron fireback. It too was hardly used.

I concluded this was the really sad part of the premises and something had to be done urgently.

The bar I knew would take some time to sort out. I checked the toilets. Everything seemed to be in order just a quick cleaning exercise. The table layout was a little more challenging. We had a combination of 2, 4 and 6 seater tables. Provision for access to the kitchen, toilets, entrance and adjoining bar had to be made. The inglenook would develop plenty of heat creating a frontal area that obviously could not be used for diners. I pondered the dilemma. Clearly, in the bar the real fire was a focal point. I felt the same should apply in the restaurant. I decided a lounge area would be ideal in the immediate inglenook vicinity. We were wondering what we would do with our old Chesterfield suite – problem solved. This in turn solved the issues of bar and entrance access. The final table layout solution fell in to place quite easily in the end. All I had to do now was enact the plan.

By the time Sara returned we had finished the restaurant re-organisation. A fire was lit and burning brightly. Light bulbs that were now working and background music completed the transformation. It was, even though I say it myself a total makeover! We were finally ready to face our busiest session. We all felt a lot more confident that we could rise to the occasion.

As was the case at lunchtime the girls worked in the kitchen, preparing the food and maintaining the restaurant service. For my part I was running the bar, albeit single-handed and taking the food orders as well. Deep down I was convinced extra support behind the bar was essential but somehow the fort had to be held in the interim. 7.00pm on the dot, bolts were drawn, outside lights switched on and we were up and running. Customers were already waiting in the car park. More new faces appeared from further afield. The pub's reputation, good or bad, seemed to be drawing a clientele from outside the hamlet. I just hoped it would continue and that we could all collectively cope.

The bar filled rapidly. Customers wanting food were automatically directed to the restaurant area. Sara would welcome them and direct them to me for drinks and food orders. Payment was taken with the order. A lesson Sue had learnt from our mutual friends Barry and Kath who ran my old local the Bricklayers Arms back in Larkfield. It would have been all too tempting to get up and leave without paying the bill for some!

One thing from my earlier visits to The Dew Drop Inn I did recall. Saturday night and Sunday lunchtimes were very busy, almost manic. Somehow we had to maintain the existing momentum, it was imperative for our survival.

The first hour flew by. I had little time to stop for anything. Customers were three deep at the bar. The slightest hiccup could spell disaster at anytime. By now, a lot of our local and regulars were in.

Smurve was sat at the bar with Tom. Smurve called for another round for the two friends.

As I went to refill Smurve's glass the tell-tale spluttering and hissing of passing gas indicated the lager had run dry. 'What a pain' I thought.

Tom, never one to be quiet on such occasions piped up 'Got a live one there boy!'

Smurve could see my frustration and plight.

Completely unprompted and without the slightest fuss he got off the bar stool and so I thought was heading for the toilet.

Tom intervened 'On yer way back boy I'll 'ave a refill!'

'Just what I need' I thought.

I felt I was losing my composure and secretively panicking. To my surprise I turned round to find Smurve behind the bar. 'Lager's on' he said. In my deepest dire moment, Smurve had not gone to the toilet, he had in fact followed round from the restaurant to the level cellar we had, gone in and changed the lager barrel. Reserve barrels were always on hand to cool down in the cellar and for a rapid changeover when empty.

I was gob smacked. 'Cheers mate'.

He responded 'Think you need an 'and 'ere? D'you want it?'

I've never been so pleased to accept assistance.

'Go for it. Thanks!'

With two of us behind the bar we soon got to grips with the surge. However the level of trade was maintained at a very high level as I suspected would be the case.

Smurve stayed behind the bar all evening. We made a good team I thought.

Later that night after closing time, and feeling totally exhausted, we had a few stalwart locals left in the bar. Both Sue and I, Sara, Tom, Smurve, Syd, Pauline and Terry sat and reflected on the earlier sessions. Thankfully we did not have a repeat performance from the previous night. It was nice to relax and have a late drink with our new found friends on our terms. Everyone served themselves as required and left the money on the bar. The tills were turned off in the event of a late visit from the 'boys in blue' that we knew would come at some point.

After a couple of extra rounds Syd and Pauline got up to leave. Syd was working an early shift the following morning on the dredger that was reclaiming sand from the Goodwin Sands for the Channel Tunnel project. Tom, Terry and Sara left at the same time. I had given Sara £20 as she left for which she was very grateful and said she would be in the following day at 11.30am. I slid a £10 note in Smurve's direction which he duly took and thanked me. We poured ourselves a final nightcap and asked Smurve if he had any bar experience. He confirmed he had helped Geoff out on occasions and helped in other pubs in the area. What good fortune – could Smurve be part of the solution to our bar staffing?

We finally locked up shortly after midnight and both retired to bed, totally exhausted. What a day!

CHAPTER 4 – Myths & Legend

Sunday lunchtime sessions are generally easy-going affairs in pubs across the land. The Dew Drop Inn was no exception to the rule. Following on from our earlier Saturday success we both hoped to continue on the front foot. Sara turned up on time as pre-arranged and immediately took charge of the restaurant preparation procedures. I had already been busy lighting both fires, attending to the cleaning and the bar re-stocking. Sue had come out of the kitchen to suggest that with it being Sunday, it might be appropriate to place roast potatoes, cheese on sticks and a few cocktail sausages on the bar for customers to help themselves to. It was meant as a goodwill gesture that Barry and Kath always maintained at the Bricklayers Arms. Barry always maintained it went down well and the punters would respond with extra beer sales.

We decided to give it a go and Sue went back to the kitchen to make the necessary preparations.

By 12.00 noon everything was ready. I opened up having taken an earlier shower and was pleased to note everything was looking fine. On instruction, Sara had put on the Cona coffee machine early and made coffee for the three of us. The smell of the freshly brewed coffee wafted through the restaurant into the bar and smelt absolutely delightful! Something else we learnt very quickly. The sense of smell is as good as sight when subliminal cravings occur. The profit margins on coffee sales are also the highest of any of our merchandise so it made sense to make it available from the start.

The first customers who arrived shortly afterwards were proof of this phenomenon. The two female members of the party ordered coffee; the accompanying men had real ale. Coffee was going to prove its worth in gold to us. As Sara confirmed, our predecessors were totally oblivious to the value of this option. High profit earning, non alcoholic and simple in use I promptly added it as a footnote to our 'specials board'.

The bar was filling quickly with customers, some locals some totally unknown.

The 'AK Gang' arrived at 12.15pm with Bob and Sal in tow. Tom, Jack and Christina were close behind. The atmosphere was building nicely as on the previous day.

As pre-arranged with Sue, bang on 12.30pm she arrived behind the bar with the 'freebie' offerings.

Bowls with cheese on sticks, cocktail sausages and the heavily salted freshly roasted potatoes went down a storm. I purposely held back half of the 'freebies' for release later in the session, an hour later. The 'AK Gang' members were right in there. They couldn't believe their luck! I overheard Tom moaning disapprovingly to Jack. 'Vultures, not seen food before etc. etc.' described the sort of comments I picked up on. I hasten to add, it didn't actually stop Tom helping himself.

The 'roasties' were obviously a novelty. I just hoped the addition of the salt would have the desired affect. It appeared too. Jim was back at the bar ordering extra AK mild on a couple of occasions with little time between rounds.

Even Tom seemed to go through his English Ale a lot quicker.

I was also pleased to note that coffee sales were proving to be very popular. I had put Sara in charge of coffee from the start. Once an order was placed and paid for, just like food orders, the order chit was passed over to Sara to deal with.

Sue was similarly kept on her toes in the kitchen. Virtually all of our visitors from outside of the hamlet were eating. Some were disappointed we did not have a Sunday roast on offer but made an alternative selection instead. It gave food for thought for future Sundays. In the meantime however, business as usual - Rome was not built in a day.

The continual comings and goings at the pub clearly confused one 'regular' more than most.

When we bought The Dew Drop Inn, Geoff and Joan the previous owners made us aware of the pub cat, Basil. They had inherited the cat with the pub when they purchased it. Basil was a neutered male, completely black and a kindred spirit of his own. Basil was evil personified. He was a working cat and recognised throughout the hamlet. His 'ratting' and 'mousing' prowess was second to none. The cat rarely needed feeding as it was self-sufficient and catered for its own fancy, as and when. Co-habiting with Jenny, Geoff's Doberman pub dog was child's play in the cat's eyes! Basil knew who was boss. Jenny did as well!

As Geoff and Joan were moving to a busy main road location they asked us to take on the cat with the pub. We agreed without question. Basil added his own brand of character to the pub. Even though a cat flap was in the back door, Basil would rarely use it.

He was far more akin to using the first floor shower room fanlight window as his means of access in all weathers, with or without his latest 'prize trophies'. I believe he had developed a liking to our shower room as an alternative feline 'dining room'. From the very start of our occupancy of the pub, we all had to expect to find the aftermath remains of mice, rats, rabbits, even hares on the shower room floor!

Basil would rarely come into the pub during opening hours for fear of being 'softened up' by cat loving customers. Regular inspections of the bar and restaurant were made at the cat's convenience. Any little indiscretions or unwanted visitors would be dealt with and despatched for the shower room floor. As a result of Basil's personal attention we rarely had a rodent problem.

Another couple of men appeared at the bar. Clive and his son Anthony Penn made their first visit of our tenure. Clive was an ex-army Major who after retirement had taken up a position as Sales Manager for a local fencing supplier. Anthony his son was actually known to me. He was the Southern Sales Representative for a national kitchen equipment manufacturer. From Anthony's reaction, the last person he expected to meet in this rural surrounding was yours truly. Having made our introductions I served the two newcomers their drinks and welcomed them to the pub.

They lived in Hassel Street the next hamlet to Bodsham Green about two miles away.

They too were partial to the AK mild although not considered to be part of the 'AK Gang'. Having seen the freebie treats on the bar they needed little encouragement to indulge.

By now there was little room left in the pub, standing room only in fact. The restaurant was predominantly full. Drinkers had discovered the Lounge area and made a beeline for the comfortable chesterfield settee and armchairs. The two girls in the restaurant/kitchen operation were handling the session well. I was similarly coping except when large rounds were being ordered.

Smurve appeared and 'fought' his way to the bar. I had pre-empted his arrival by pouring his pint of Fosters in advance. 'Have that with me Smurve. Thanks again for last night!' He took a long hard draw on the lager. 'No problem mate. Anytime I can help. Just give me the nod'

That was just what I had hoped for. When things got out of hand I had someone I could call on I thought.

Slowly but surely I felt we were coming to terms with our new venture. I was a little disturbed to note a couple of cars pulling up onto the green and driving off. I concluded the occupants obviously thought we were too busy and decided to move on elsewhere. It was one of the problems of becoming a successful operation to contend with, but that would hopefully be in the future.

Bang on 1.30pm Sara appeared with the second round of 'freebies' that Sue had prepared. They hardly touched the bar before they were being ravenously devoured. It was a bit of an eye opener! However, rounds of beer seemed to be just as quickly re-ordered so I concluded it was definitely the right thing to do.

The remaining time of the lunchtime session passed uneventfully. The level of trade remained high right up to calling time at 2.30pm. It was a relief to sit down and put my feet up. The bar was rapidly thinning out so I went customer side and had a chat with Tom and Smurve. Both men commented that they hadn't seen the level of business we had just experienced ever in Geoff's era. Tom bought a final round to celebrate.

Sue and Sara came to join us for their 'wind down' drink in the bar after finishing up in the kitchen. It had been a very good session. Shortly afterwards everyone left. We were so tired we retired to bed for an afternoon knap as seems to be customary in the trade so to do.

6.00pm and we woke in a minor panic. The pub was due to open in an hour and there was plenty to be done before then! The 'siesta' we had just taken did us a power of good. I went downstairs in a different frame of mind completely and finished up the remaining glass washing and re-bottled the bar. Both fires had died down to a smoulder so new logs were put on and in no time the flames were dancing again. A rapid clearance of ashtrays followed by a quick wipe over of the bar and tables and we were pretty well ready for business. I decided a quick hoover through was in order to finally complete the presentation of the bar and restaurant area. A quick visit in to the kitchen to switch on the fryers for pre-heating and I was done. Sue in the meantime had dolled herself up and went down to open up whilst I had a quick change and freshen up.

We had agreed in advance to have a role reversal that evening. We didn't really know what to expect at this stage. By mutual agreement Sara was not coming in to work on Sunday evenings so we were on our own. The role change was also meant to allow customers to meet both of us. The kitchen staff members were rarely seen by the regulars so we both felt it necessary to make the effort to be equally seen. From a selfish point of view it enabled me to be seen 'customer' side of the bar as well. All too often one hears of landlords who hide themselves away in their ivory towers, never socializing with the punters. Bearing in mind the punters provide the landlord's living not to be seen with them would be a sure recipe for disaster.

By 7.15pm we had our first customers. Some were regulars and some were new faces. Clive and Anthony had come down for an early game of darts as was their normal early Sunday evening pastime. Another guy entered the bar and joined them, obviously well known to each other. Phil Dense, Clive' nephew lived in the cottage opposite. He was a young and successful city stockbroker. His parents lived in the Old Vicarage on the top of the hill opposite the little hamlet school

Clive bought his nephew his half of Carlsberg lager which Phil was very particular about. The three of them monopolised the dartboard in the lower saloon bar area. It was in fact the only pub game facility we had. There was no pool table, fruit machine or juke box in our establishment. We did possess a pack of cards, a cribbage board and a set of dominoes under the bar. To my knowledge, they were unused and in the same place for the full time we owned The Dew Drop Inn! Being such a friendly establishment our pub characters provided the entertainment. Everyone conversed with each other and any strangers that came in.

Molly and Terry came across having successfully coerced Mrs. Rose to baby sit their two youngsters. The two took their places at the bar. Molly was keen to discuss something with us. She had heard from Mrs. Rose that Sara had started part time work with us at the pub. She was keen to know if there were any other opportunities or positions available.

Both Sue and I listened intently to Molly's request.

We were both very interested as Sara was strictly limited to weekends and with her oncoming examination timetable even those hours at times may be in question.

I had to retire to the kitchen to prepare two meals of Jumbo cod, chips and peas. This gave me a little time to mull over what had just been discussed. It struck me that it was more than likely that both women could be employed. My only reservation was the level of trade really needed to be established before committing to Molly.

I served the fish and chip meals to the expectant customers and went back to Terry and Molly at the bar. I confirmed our interest to Molly but explained our dilemma regarding the level of business. The last thing either of us wanted was to take on staff only to lay them back of again because the level of business could not sustain their employment. Molly was completely understanding of the situation and was perfectly happy to wait. I was called away for another food order preparation which gave Sue the opportunity to talk about the children and other mutual matters.

Tom appeared with Bob and his wife Sal. Tom was surprised to be greeted by the good lady wife behind the bar. Taking his usual 'perch' he was most impressed to be served his usual ale with his dedicated pot by Sue without having to utter a word. I had trained Sue well in the short time we had been in The Dew Drop Inn.

'Bloody 'ell girl! What you done wiv' the old boy?' he asked gruffly.

Sue was in the middle of pouring Tom's brother's Guinness and duly responded

'He's in the kitchen tonight. He'll be out soon.'

'That's bloody women's work!' Tom spouted out and went for his pot.

If looks cold kill! Every female pair of eyes were trained on the man at the end of the bar. Piercing and menacing looks from all directions. Tom had revealed his chauvinistic side and very publicly at that. In a fit of uneasiness he pulled out his trusted tobacco pouch, filled the pipe, lit the contents and tried to hide within the enormous cloud of aromatic smoke he had just created.

I came back in to the bar with part of the food order, returning to the kitchen for the rest. I sensed the pretty cold atmosphere that prevailed in the bar.

Tom was the first to break the silence. 'Are you alright boy? Dinner lady tonight eh?' he taunted me.

Not having been privy to the previous incident I didn't take too much notice of Tom's jibe.

'Fair do's Tom. The old girl's been out there all lunch time. I'm giving her a break!'

'No offence meant. When yer ready gal!' Tom tapped his pot 'Best get all this lot a drink as well' referring to the four others sat at the bar. 'What ever you're 'aving as well Sue! Best have one for the ol' boy too!' Tom always felt buying a round would solve most issues.

In the main they did even though it took a little time to work. He was always generous when it came to paying his way.
Sue did the honours and I returned to sit with the good lady behind the bar.
The three dart players finished their game and took to the bar stools at the lower saloon bar end. I moved down to take up conversation with them, and just in time to serve another round.
9.00pm was not far off. Significant to me because that was the latest time food orders would be taken. Fryers could then be switched off, surfaces cleared, washing up completed and the kitchen swabbed through before closing down. The limited food orders that night meant the procedure was completed pretty quickly. Having attended to the kitchen closedown I was then able to return to the bar. I turned off the restaurant lights signifying its closure.
Back in the bar Clive and Anthony had left but been replaced by Smurve and Rod. Jake and Evil Emma also made an appearance as they normally did on a Sunday evening.
Emma loved to reminisce over the past with anyone who was willing to listen. Off duty and anxious to please I returned to the bar area, customer-side and sat with Jake and Emma. They were both very receptive in conversation and were clearly happy with the minor changes that we had effected in our short occupancy.
I got the distinct impression they were not over keen on the previous owners. The conversation moved on and Emma completely out of the blue asked bluntly
'Have you seen the 'White Lady' yet?'
I hadn't got a clue what she was on about.
'Right here, in the corner opposite the entrance.' She continued. Clearly she was pretty well fired up and wasn't going to give up without an answer.
'No I've not seen anything!' I replied quizzically.
Jake in the meantime had left us and moved over to talk with Tom. He had obviously heard the story before.
Apparently Evil Emma was in earlier days a member of a local white witch coven. Anything to do with the supernatural was of great importance too her.
In no time at all she tried to convince me of the spiritual presence. Apparently way back in the mist of time when the pub was three cottages and the middle cottage was the 'bar', some sort of extra marital association was taking place between the lady of the middle

cottage and the male counterpart of one of the outer cottages.
Rumour has it the husband in the middle cottage came home unexpectedly to catch the other two in a compromising position. The truth was out! The husband flew into a blind rage and started a fight with his wife's lover. The fight became more and more violent. In a desperate effort to quell the violence, the wife threw herself between the two duelling men. In so doing she was stabbed through the heart by her lover and died instantly. The fatal blow was due to have been received by the husband, but alas, fate decreed a different outcome. The 'White Lady' appears periodically as a wispy apparition in the corner of the bar. Emma relished telling her account. Unfortunately, being a non-believer in ghosts and the super-natural I was not particularly impressed. I am a firm believer that technology can provide an answer to the vast majority of these occurrences. However to play along with Emma's belief I showed as much interest as possible at her revelation. Thankfully she accepted my alleged interest without question.

I bought Jake and Emma a refill of their glasses which went down well.

By this time Emma was in full flow.

'Of course, years ago this old pub had a blacker side to its history. Old man Demsett had the pub in the early 60's and had his ties to the London mobsters you know?'

Suddenly I was a lot more interested.

Apparently, Bill Demsett was well attached to the likes of the Cray twins, other South London mob leaders and no less than the Great Train Robbers. Lorries would be seen arriving in the dead of night, unloading and leaving under the cover of darkness. All seemed very sinister and clandestine to say the least. Ronnie Biggs the most notorious Great Train Robber and his sidekick Buster were said to have used the pub on many occasions. Furthermore, Emma revealed the local myth that the Great Train Robbery was partly planned in The Dew Drop Inn and by virtue of its remote position the non-recovered proceeds and equipment were stored and subsequently disposed of from here.

What a story I thought to myself as Emma recounted the very last detail. What if we were sitting on the un-discovered fortune?

Tom brought us back to reality. Requesting another round he duly announced the 'poppycock' surrounding Emma's ramblings. I wasn't going to disagree, but similarly it did strike me as being a little far fetched. For the time being I decided the legend would be left unproven. However I would be on the look out for any proof in the days and months ahead. Emma took everything in her stride, feeling her neighbourly duty had been fulfilled.

Time was moving on and the good lady rang time for closure with her party piece announcement:

'C'mon all you good people and you others, let the landlord get to bed with his wife!'

The hint was duly taken and the customers drank up and left the pub. We closed up and turned the lights off and retired. We had managed to navigate our business through the first choppy waters with reasonable success. There were bigger hills to climb in the future. Shortly after midnight, the pub was spot checked by the local policeman with his sergeant in tow. They found the establishment in darkness and left satisfied that the licensing hours were being adhered too.

CHAPTER 5 – Here Comes Trouble!

The following few days brought us down to earth with a bump. The trade level plummeted from the previous days of the week. In fairness our predecessors didn't open on Mondays at all, nor did they open for Tuesday lunchtimes so it would obviously take time for the news that we were open to filter through the 'grapevine'. The quiet spell was a welcome relief and gave much needed time to attend to those little jobs that needed doing after moving home. Unpacking our own house contents had been completely overlooked since moving in, other than the bare essentials to survive - there just weren't enough hours in the day to be business owner and homemaker together.

At the start of the new week, the usual bar preparation and cleaning routines were completed as normal. We decided the bar would be opened as normal but rarely were any customers visiting before 1.00pm. On Monday mornings this was quite fortuitous. We became accustomed to receiving our dray delivery from the Phoenix brewery, normally late morning and also our frozen food supplier would make the first of two deliveries during the week. The second would normally follow on Thursday which was ideal to allow proper stock rotation and availability.

This day the dray was first to deliver. The draymen knew the routine and their way around as they had delivered to the previous owners requiring very little in the way of input from me. Having a level cellar meant deliveries could be handled efficiently, easily and with minimal physical effort. Basement cellars were a totally different proposition. We weren't a high turnover beer pub so the draymen finished pretty quickly. It was customary to offer the draymen a drink once they had finished their task which I duly did. I have often wondered how the dray driver gets on. If a drink is taken at every pub delivered too the driver would probably be many times over the top by the end of his round! Still it was not my problem.

The extra time we had on our hands enabled us to consider future plans and routines. In between spasmodic customer visits day to day procedures could be decided upon. Mondays would become our banking day. Cash, till rolls and safe contents would be reconciled and surpluses taken to the local bank in Wye.

A simple task in its own rights to perform, but one that was essential and would take at least three hours to complete. The bank visit would also be 'dualled' with a town visit to Ashford for Cash and Carry purchases. Those items that we found were essential to the running of our business but were not available for direct delivery. Tobacco, paper and cleaning products immediately sprung to mind. It was still early spring and Mother Nature was yet to get the new growing season into gear. I took the opportunity to check out the garden areas to the pub. Our private garden to the rear was clearly well overgrown and had been un-attended for some time. The lawn turf was tufted and sadly in need of treatment. The beer garden alongside the car park, extending to the rear of the premises was in better condition although in desperate need of a first cut. The trestle tables were only good for scrapping at the earliest opportunity. The total area extended to about one and a half acres. Mowing would probably be needed twice a week in the season. Clearly my small domestic mower would be totally inadequate for the job. A new mowing machine would be required to serve the purpose.

As I had a little time on my hands and customers were very thin on the ground I decided to at the least show willing and took my little Flymo mower out, blew off the winter cobwebs and had a go at mowing the beer garden. It was hard going although taking a little pass at a time meant we were getting there. The only customers we had during that lunchtime session were dealt with by the wife. Only a few pints at best which proved to be useful as it enabled me to at least make the beer garden more presentable sporting its first cut of the season. It made an immediate impression. The shorter grass smartened the external area up and complimented the olde worlde exterior and charm of The Dew Drop Inn. Furthermore it highlighted the poor state of the trestle benches. Something had to be done urgently to preserve the good image.

No time like the present. I put away the mower, went indoors to let Sue knew my intentions and left the pub with a view to doing the banking, finding a new mower and trestle benches. It was actually the first time I had left the premises since we had moved there. It was nice to have a break. I first went into Wye and did the banking. From there I went via the back lanes through Brook to a garden centre on the Folkestone Road, east of Ashford.

Strongman mowers sub-contracted sales space in the garden centre and it wasn't long before I had found just what I was looking for. A

13.5 horsepower multi-purpose mower tractor with three blade cutting deck, powered grass collector and trailer - just the job! The mini tractor was available ex-stock so I negotiated a good discount and made the purchase. Delivery would be made the following day. That solved that little problem. The garden trestle issue was not quite so easy to solve. The garden centre had access to suppliers of the trestle benches but the excessive prices deterred me. Even with the sizeable order I wished to place, the discount on offer was totally unacceptable and the cost way too high. As I was leaving, one of the yardmen approached me. He said he had seen the interest I had been showing in the various trestle benches on offer. He gathered the price was a key issue and the reason I was leaving so soon. He explained a cousin of his manufactured equivalent products in Hothfield, a small village on the other side of town. He further maintained the prices his relative charged were only a fraction of those charged by the garden centre. I thanked him and as time was not pressing headed for Hothfield.

I found the yardman's cousin's workshop. It was something like a scene from the hillbillies. Four dungaree clad men with tartan style lumberjack shirts were working there. All bar one had long, greying, full face beards. Malcolm introduced himself as the owner. I explained about my previous visit to the garden centre and my encounter with his purported cousin. This was all duly confirmed and I went on to explain my needs. Malcolm took me to one of the adjoining sheds in which there was a massive array of trestle benches, tables, chairs and other garden paraphernalia. By sheer fluke I had found exactly what I was looking for. The prices shown were indeed as his cousin stated, and very much lower than the garden centre. I explained to Malcolm I was looking for four six seater and six four seater trestle benches initially. I was offered a discount amounting to 15% off the price. This I felt was okay but decided to push for a little more. By increasing the order by three further four seaters I twisted Malcolm's arm to increase the discount to 20% and throw in free delivery. I confirmed the order and paid a third deposit, the balance paid on delivery. The delivery was planned to be made no later than mid-day the following Thursday. I was delighted with my shopping expedition and returned to tell Sue all about it.

On my return I found the pub closed. I went round the back to find Sue hanging washing on the outside line. She said things had continued to be quiet through the whole lunchtime session. A couple of phone calls had been taken from various suppliers. One however was of interest to me.

Phillip was a representative of a real ale distributor and had heard of the change of ownership. He was in the area the following day and wanted to make a courtesy call and show us the products he could offer. Real ale was of particular interest to me. In former times my former business partner and I had made many a visit to rural pubs sporting some of the old favoured names in the quest of real ale excellence. Harveys, Youngs, Wadworths, Theakstons, Fullers to name but a few, all brewers of excellent real ales. They all carried a pedigree of their own exemplified by their stable of wonderful ales. CAMRA was the organisation that supported and encouraged the real ale tradition in favour of modern chemical lager production. Lager was rapidly becoming taken up by today's younger drinkers. I was one publican who wanted to make a stand against the modern trend, indeed do all in my power to reverse it!

I rang Phillip back and made arrangements for a meeting in closed hours the following day.

The rest of the day I spent destroying the old trestle benches. Two were still serviceable so were spared the fate of the big hammer and the fire I started at the bottom of the garden. Unfortunately the wood was very wet and not suitable to burn on the inglenooks. It took a lot to get the fire going. A cocktail of red diesel and petrol did the trick finally. The girls came home from school and the enchantment of a bonfire amused them no end, helping me for the remainder of daylight hours.

Whilst the fire was burning I took the opportunity to clear the remains of the garage and dispose of the rubbish on the fire. Similarly, years of accumulation of old fence panels, pallets and garden waste were collected and disposed of in the same way. By the time we finished the garden was more akin to a beer garden although the trestle benches were vastly depleted in the short term. The following weekend was the first of the May bank holidays which I had hoped the business trade could benefit from. Obviously the weather was a major consideration. This was the driving reason for insisting on a garden furniture delivery in advance of the weekend. It never ceases to amaze me how observant country-folk seem to be. The initial garden maintenance and improvements were the talking point in the pub that evening.

Rod and Smurve called in fairly early, to be joined by Terry who had a late finish. They all commented about the difference even under the external lighting. Two of the four students frequented the pub as well. That represented the sole trade that evening and I decided to save on electricity by closing at 10.00pm after everyone had left. The daily till taking was miserable to say the least.

An early night proved to be beneficial for both of us. The next day I was up and going about my chores with a new purpose in life. Fortunately I didn't have to wait too long after completing the bar preparations. I had just poured our morning coffee when a knock at the front door was heard. I answered to find the Strongman mower man come to deliver my new 'toy'. The gleaming new red Wheelhorse tractor was driven down the ramps out of the van. What a machine! The powered glass collector was already fitted so the trailer was loose. The delivery driver then took time to demonstrate the operation of the machine.

I set the driver a challenge asking him to mow a section of our rear private garden. Not a problem whatsoever. In fact the main issue was the effectiveness of the powered grass collector. In no time at all the collection hopper was full and needed emptying. The finished grass cut was absolutely brilliant. I stopped the demonstrator, gave him the cheque balance, thanked him and sent him on his way. I wanted a go before having to retire to run the bar. Fifteen minutes later the job was done and we were very spick and span! I parked up the new machine and trailer in the cleared garage and thought it prudent to remove the powered grass collector for the time being, enabling the use of the trailer with the tractor to collect and transport logs from the distant log heap and store. This addition would be a great assistance. Till now I had to use my very old and decrepit wheelbarrow. The trailer would carry six times the amount of logs to that of the wheelbarrow. Playtime was now over and work beckoned as a couple of vehicles drew onto the car park.

I went in via the rear entrance and was greeted in the bar by Colin and Suzanne and another woman who I was introduced to. Colin ordered the usual for Suzanne and himself and a coffee for their guest who transpired to be a senior figure in the Newfoundland Society.

With little more time spent in serving the drinks Suzanne eagerly asked if Sue and I had considered Newfoundland dog ownership further. I must confess to being caught a little on the hop at

Suzanne's direct question. She went on stating that time was of the essence in such matters and that faint-hearted approaches would rarely succeed. At this point I stopped her, went and got Sue and returned to hear the rest of her rendition.

Apparently, the Newfoundland Society is quite particular at who and where dogs of this breed are housed. The owners are vetted in advance because of the larger than normal expense involved in owning this type of dog and the size and type of home the owners can offer. The Society does not have legal powers to prevent ownership, but as and when difficulties in ownership appear that could impact on the dog's welfare the Society in conjunction with the RSPCA is quick to act. Re-homing can then follow. Suzanne went straight to the point. Margaret Simpson from the Newfoundland Society had been charged to re-house two 'Newfee's' that had been rescued from an address in the East End of London. The owner was completely incapable or resourced to have one, let alone two of these magnificent creatures. Margaret went on to say that Roscoe and Rachel were brother and sister and if possible they would like to home the two together. Would we be interested? Naturally the dogs would need to be inspected by a vet and treated for any pre-existing conditions and given a 'makeover' before being handed over. It was a big commitment and time was of the essence.

Without hesitation we said we were interested. Margaret asked to have a quick tour of the establishment and the grounds. Sue accompanied her I stayed in the bar Colin had another drink.

'What do you really think Patrick?'

'Brilliant!' I replied 'Just a little surprised its double bubble but there you are. The girls will be overjoyed.'

Suzanne voiced her opinion 'It's heaven here for any dog. East London's no place for Newfees.'

Colin took out a cigarette and lit up.

A mere five minutes later, Margaret and Sue returned to the bar. Like Suzanne, Margaret felt the facilities we could offer would be nothing short of doggy heaven.

'Right then, no time to waste!' she exclaimed 'I'll be back down tomorrow with the dogs' she addressed Colin and Suzanne directly. 'It's been so nice meeting you both. I'll leave you with Suzanne and Colin to sort the final points.' Margaret left shortly after finishing her coffee.

'I'll ring as soon as Roscoe and Rachel are with us. You can come up and see them then. If you are happy then we'll get Mike Potter the vet to check them over. He's great with big dogs, the best. Then a quick manicure, pedicure and shampoo and they'll be ready for their new home.' Suzanne explained to Sue.

'We are both looking forward to it!' Sue replied.

Colin and Suzanne stayed for lunch. They both had ham, eggs and chips for which they were very complimentary. This I found bizarre as Tom had informed me, on the quiet, that Colin and Suzanne both frequented the Bull Inn quite often as well.

A few other customers used our service that session. They were not locals and had come across us by accident. They had come out from Canterbury and stayed for a snack lunch. Asking if we did Sunday roast lunches reminded me of how essential it was to sort this out. Sunday roasts are relatively easy for catering. They carry high appeal and a price premium to match. Good meat and fresh vegetable sources were imperative for a successful operation.

The Canterbury party left saying they would be back. I said roast Sunday lunches would be coming soon, probably by the late May Bank Holiday that was following four weeks later.

Colin and Suzanne left shortly afterwards saying they would be in touch.

I duly shut the bar and closed up.

I spent a little time in the bar and cellar. We currently had two hand-pumped draught real ales. I was trying to find bar space to increase our capability to six or seven real ales. The bigger the selection, the more attractive it became to the CAMRA enthusiast. I was prepared to sacrifice some of the keg draught beers that were not so popular. Once I established we had immediate space for three extra real ale pumps I had to turn my attention to the cellarage aspects of the proposed change. The cellar was very small and confined. It was temperature controlled environment cooled by a blast chiller. This advantage meant that fresh and chilled food could also be stored in the room as well. The disadvantage was clearly the room was so small for what was expected of it. Traditional Real ale stillage storage is unfortunately not that space efficient as compared to that of keg beers.

Finding the extra space for the new beer casks was going to be difficult. As I was pondering the dilemma the door bell rang.

Philip the representative from West Country Products was, as pre-arranged on the doorstep for our appointment. I invited him into the bar. After formal introductions were completed we got down to business. He had never heard of the pub before and so it was his first visit. He had only come across the change of ownership after being informed from his head office of the grant of our protection order. Drink suppliers have their own 'grapevine' and so Philip acted on the lead. I took him on a rapid tour of the trade areas. He was suitably impressed and loved the potential for expanding his trade portfolio. Once I explained my intention to increase the real ale portfolio in the pub Phillip started his sales patter. He had a catalogue listing a fantastic range of real ales and beers from all over the country. There were names well known too me but the vast majority totally unheard of. Phillip gave some sound advice and recommendations of beers that had a cult following and that the pub could benefit from. He also offered some highly favourable inducements and a far better discount structure than offered by Phoenix. I was prepared to run with him but for the potential cellar storage issue.

Upon making a closer inspection of the cellar Philip recommended moving away from traditional ale 'stillage' where casks are stored on their side in favour of modern 'spear' techniques. The spear is the modern method of dispensing ales used in conjunction with old fashioned hand pump beer engines. I must confess to being totally ignorant of the new system and soon realised this was not only the solution to my dilemma but improved wastage and profitability should follow. Using the 'spear' means the casks are stored on end and can be stacked. The beer is drawn through a clever tap arrangement that allows the beer to be spiled (allowed to breath) and extracted at the same time. I immediately agreed to make the change of system and switch our real ale supply to West Country Products. Phillip was delighted and took an immediate order for four new ales. He quickly went out to his van and returned with four hand pump engines, four spear assemblies, a coil of pipe and promotional pump clips to advertise the new beers. He also supplied me with signage, promotional literature, product lists and some beer mats in addition. All I had to do was re-organise my cellar space pipe up the spear assemblies and connect to the hand pumps installed on the bar. Furthermore as a final gratuity Philip agreed to supply the new ales on a buy two get third free basis as an aid to getting the new beers off the ground. Philip left after a quick cup of tea stating the new order would be delivered on the next dray delivery in my area which was scheduled for the following Friday. Ideal for the bank holiday weekend I thought. Having said farewell to my new acquaintance I set about the task in hand. It took me the remainder of the afternoon to re-pipe the two existing real ales and switch them to 'spears'. The saving in space in the cellar was amazing. I had to leave the two other pumps for the following day as the time to open was rapidly nearing.

Customers were again very thin on the ground that evening. I spent a lot of the time busying myself in the cellar carrying out the preparatory works for the following day's new installation work whilst keeping an eye on the bar and serving the occasional customers that called in. Having done what I could in the cellar I turned my attention to the soft drinks storage area that housed all the electrical metering and fuse boxes. One thing Geoff made me aware of was the tendency of the pub to be forced to close when power cuts were experienced. This struck me at the time as a little odd. Modern pub businesses are totally reliant on a fully maintained power supply. As we were rural, our power was delivered by overhead power lines that were obviously highly susceptible to wind and storm damage, as were the other dwellings in the hamlet. Our dependence on power being maintained was all the more critical as the tills, cellar blaster, freezers, kitchen equipment, lighting and central heating controls were electrically powered. Relief was at hand as I retained one of my former company large standby generators for such mains power down situations. There would however need to be a change in the wiring to accommodate the new emergency appliance. I took the quiet time to check the wiring and formulate the new 'changeover' system that would be required. All appeared to be straightforward enough so I prepared a parts list for collection from an electrical wholesalers next time we were in town. This important addition meant more expense, but would mean the pub would become a haven for local inhabitants and customers alike when power supplies were interrupted. We subsequently found out it was a very prudent move as during our tenure of ownership power loss was a very regular occurrence and the pub became the hub of the community. The generator allowed us to continue as normal at such times.

As on the previous night I closed early as there appeared little interest being shown. No point in blatantly wasting time, fuel and energy.
The following day, having concluded the entire bar preparatory procedures promptly, I went back to checking out the electric circuitry. The inspection I made the previous evening revealed a few concerns and irregularities. Being such an old building there were countless circuits that had been altered or extended over time. Some had been completed professionally, some in a most amateur and DIY fashion. In the worst case an extra fryer had been wired in to the kitchen using bell wire. I was amazed the wiring had remained intact for as long as it had. A fryer is a high consuming appliance and should be supplied through ring main cabling. This was something, I concluded, had to be remedied as soon as possible. As luck would have it I had the proper cable to hand and decided to rewire there and then. It only took an hour or so to complete, but the ramifications of a premature cable failure in a building of this age played on my mind. Sparks, dust and old, dry timber don't get on well with each other. The threat of fire has always been one of my serious hang-ups in life and the potential personal risk to members of my family. Having made this earlier revelation I decided it may be prudent to get an electrician in and professionally test and check the pub wiring.
Completely without warning my first customer of the day appeared in the bar. It was Tom. The weather had again turned inclement and Tom came home as a result. Unbeknown to me Tom had been in the bar for a while.
'Morning boy! Got trouble with the ol' leccy then?' he enquired 'Not surprised, the world and his dog's had a go at it over the years!'
I duly served Tom his English Ale and pot.
'So it seems old man!' I replied.
I explained to Tom my earlier remedial work and the discovery of the bell wired fryer.
Tom tutted in sympathy.
'Still you've fixed it now, eh Boy?' He downed the remains of his beer in one. Tom was obviously thirsty. I replenished his beer forthwith.
'Bloody awful weather again, mate' He went on having drawn out his tobacco pouch and pipe and started filling the bowl.
'Yeah! Who'd have thought it's May in a few days.' I replied.
Tom stoked up his pipe. The aromatic smoke was lovely.

'Tell you what! I'll give you a hand this afternoon when you close. How's that sound boy? Keep me from getting under Helen's feet.'
It was a genuine offer and one I was very grateful of. On these occasions two heads are better than one and the work is completed so much quicker with two people on the job.
'See you've mown the lawns then! You ain't hanging about boy, unlike that old lazy bugger Geoff. He never did anything!'
I then went into describing my new tractor mower purchase. Tom being very 'machine-minded' listened intently and showed real interest in my new toy. So much so we both went out to the garage to view the little beauty.
Tom was really impressed and remarked on how heavy duty engineered the tractor appeared to be.
We returned to the bar as a couple of customers pulled onto the car park. They entered the bar and ordered coffee and ploughman's lunches. Not a lot but every little helped.
The phone rang and was answered by Sue who was now busy in the kitchen. Shortly afterwards, she appeared behind the bar to tell me she was going out. Suzanne had just rung to say the dogs had arrived from London. Sue left quickly. She was on an exciting mission. No time to lose!
I decided there was little point in keeping the bar open. The earlier visitors had left, leaving just Tom and me in the bar. I shut and locked the front door and we got on with the business in hand.
The bar canopy lighting was fluorescent tube fittings that Tom thought had been installed by the previous owners to Geoff. They were hideous and had obviously been a DIY installation. They were too bright and totally out of character and after joint agreement had to go. I had some very nice down lighters left over from a previous project in our earlier home. We both agreed they would be far more suitable and with dimmer switches fitted could be adjusted to suit the required ambience. On examination the existing fittings were wired in bell wire. Could this be the same person responsible for the earlier fryer bodge? More than likely we concluded.
I went into the rear soft drinks store and tripped out the lighting circuit breaker. The bar went dark and gloomy. I started to check the cabling to find it was alright except between the control switches and fittings.
Tom in the meantime had cleared all the glasses and tankards from the racking to gain access to the light fittings. At this point I removed

the switch covers to gain access to the wiring terminals for disconnection. I started to undo the terminals and went to pull the cables out from the terminal blocks only to be shocked and 'thrown' to the end of the bar.

'Bloody 'ell! Are you alright boy?' Tom asked whilst showing his concern.

'Sodding thing's still live!' I exclaimed. Knowing that the lights had gone out when the circuit breakers were turned off I hardly believed what I had just said. 'It can't possibly be!' I thought to myself.

I rummaged through my toolbox for my neon tester. I applied the tester across the supposed live terminals to which it indicated no charge whatsoever. It was dead as a dodo.

For the second time I went and touched the cable to remove it from its connector and again for the second time found myself shocked and thrown down the bar.

'Sod this!' I uttered out loud.

Tom couldn't believe his eyes. 'It must still be live!' he commented.

'No chance. Something very strange here Tom' I said as I got up and went out the back again. This time I was not chancing anything. I withdrew all three company fuses from their carriers. The mains supply was now totally isolated from the building. The whole building was in an eerie silence as everything electrical stopped working.

Tom popped over to his home and returned with his Megameter. It was the most sensitive metering device available. On his return he touched the bare wires and terminals. No readings were shown. The circuits were totally dead.

Armed with this knowledge I set about the disconnection procedure again, only to find myself 'electrocuted' again and thrown down the bar for the third time. My patience was now wearing thin. In silence I took out my insulating tape, wrapped it around the exposed parts of the screwdriver and decided to treat the operation as a 'live operation' from there on in.

Tom by now could only see the funny side of the situation. For my part I just went ahead pretending all the wires were live and ensuring I didn't make contact with any of them, even though I knew they were dead. It was bizarre.

Two hours later the works were complete.

New down lighters with controlling dimmers had been fitted, and the associated wiring replaced in proper lighting cable. The circuits tested and the power re-instated. The job was well done, even though no explanation for the live cabling could be given.

The finished effect was really pleasing. The light was warmer and far more suited to the Olde Worlde charm of the bar area.

We celebrated with English Ales and Real Ale for the workers.

To this day I am unable to offer any scientific explanation to what had occurred that afternoon. Tom witnessed the occurrences and remained just as baffled.

Darkness was falling as the good lady wife re-appeared. She was delighted with our afternoon's efforts; she was not so resolute about her own. She joined us in the bar and started to tell me about the two Newfee's she had been to see. Tears welled up in her eyes as she recounted her earlier visit. Mike Potter the vet was there at the same time making his examination. Both dogs were apparently in a very poor state of health. They had both been allegedly locked in a 6' x 4' garden shed for weeks on end. Not fed, watered or exercised had played a major nightmare in both dog's minds. They were totally emaciated and in a terrible state. Amazingly they hadn't fought each other and become cannibalistic in any way. However, Mike Potter's examination highlighted serious psychological trauma in Rachel's behaviour and it was felt putting her to sleep was the only humane solution. This plan of action was enacted leaving just Roscoe to be homed.

Un-deterred by what Sue had just recounted I was disappointed to hear of Rachel's demise but all the more certain that Roscoe should come to join our family. With our two daughters support I was convinced we could rebuild his existence and erase his bad memories of his previous life.

Sue rang Colin back to tell him of our agreement to re-home Roscoe. He was delighted and said he would pop down for a celebratory drink that night and conclude the formalities then.

We were both unanimous in our decision and decided to tell the girls of the impending canine arrival that night.

Tom duly drained his pot content and left saying he would be back later. For my part I decided to put my feet up for a while and relax. It had been quite a trying day so far!

Sue woke me at 6.45pm from a deep sleep. I had been watching the television but found that I dozed off in the comfort of an armchair. Time had just slipped by and it was a rush to meet the normal opening time. A swift wash and freshen up, change of clothes and I was off downstairs. Sue had helped by stoking the fire in the bar and put a couple of logs on. The flames were building nicely as I flicked the outside lights on and opened the front door. As I went back into the bar I could get the full nightime effect of the lighting changes made earlier. It was an amazing transformation which I was really pleased with.

I didn't have to wait long for the first customers. Sara appeared in the bar with her then boyfriend Martin who she introduced too me. Martin was a likable chap who worked in a local Builders Merchants in Ashford and was a couple of years older than Sara. He was looking for extra evening and weekend work and asked if there were any opportunities at The Dew Drop Inn behind the bar. I asked if he had any experience, only to learn that his parents were the owners and proprietors of a nice restaurant in Wye and that he had worked with them but restaurant and waiting work was not really to his liking. Pub bar work was more interesting.

With the looming Bank Holiday weekend I decided a trial period could be worked this coming weekend. If it was successful we could firm up arrangements thereafter. Initially, I offered Matt hours that would coincide with Sara's working arrangements and an initial rate of pay that was acceptable. Matt was grateful and agreed to my proposal. Friday night would be his first shift. I suggested he should come at 6.00pm to be shown the ropes! I bought them both a drink to seal the deal.

Shortly afterwards and to his word, Tom came in. Like me he was very favourably surprised at the new lighting effect we had created earlier that afternoon. I stood Tom his first English Ale as a token of appreciation of his help which was gratefully received. He engaged in conversation with his niece and her boyfriend.

Colin and Suzanne appeared shortly afterwards. They were both over the moon that we had decided to take Roscoe on. Suzanne was keen to speak to Sue to update her of Roscoe's progress.

He had been bathed and shampooed initially to treat his poor skin condition and his overgrown claws trimmed. His coat had been trimmed to remove all the matted fur followed by another cosmetic shampooing and blow drying. Suzanne assured Sue she wouldn't recognise Roscoe as the dog she had seen earlier. He was now receiving a proper nutritious diet and it was hoped his sad background was well and truly behind him. Before Mike Potter left he had administered booster injections to the dog so there was no reason for delaying Roscoe's move. Suzanne had suggested that Roscoe could be transferred to us on the Saturday morning which I was not in favour of. Bank holiday weekends could be funny times; you're either manically busy or dead quiet. There was no way of knowing. Taking delivery of the dog in the middle of this unknown worried me. We therefore agreed to take him a day earlier in the hope he would settle quickly. With the matter decided Colin decided to settle in for some serious drinking. Suzanne was doing the driving that night regardless!

Some what surprisingly Phil entered the bar a little later. He was normally a weekend customer, staying in digs during the week in London. However, as he later explained, the imminence of the bank holiday weekend had lured him from the 'smoke' as he had decided upon an extended break. The markets were relatively quiet he maintained so home he came. He wasn't sure but he thought that his brother Edward, Ed to those who knew him, could well be home as well. Ed was an agricultural student in his final year of his degree course at a college in the West Country. Final exam time for Ed was only a matter of weeks away and Phil thought he may opt to come home for revision and only return to take the exams as required.

Somewhat out of character and much to Tom's delight Syd and Pauline came in for a drink. They were both impressed with the new lighting arrangements. It was also quite fortuitous for me because I really needed to consult Syd on two professional matters. Having served them their drinks I beckoned to Syd to come down to the lower bar.

I had previously noted that the massive chestnut support column between the two bars was showing signs of splitting. Not apparently too serious at this point, but as this member carried major floor and roof loading from above I certainly wanted to prevent any further degrading. This is where I thought Syd could help.

Having described the problem to Syd, he initially thought of bolting carefully positioned plates to tie the column together. Whilst this undoubtedly would work I was concerned with the aesthetics. I thought it was a repair that would be totally out of character and unsightly. I suggested as an alternative to make up three steel strip 'girdles' that could be pre-heated and then welded around the chestnut column which on cooling would contract, hence tighten and close the splitting. It would be a neater and debatably more effective solution to the problem. Furthermore, I was very keen to have a wrought iron screen divider made and fitted between the bars. Upon hearing my ideas Syd immediately volunteered his services and confirmed his interest. He would pop up in the next few days to take a few dimensions and finally agree a design for the screening. It was certainly becoming a very productive day.

The evening was passing off quite well. For midweek our level of business was most encouraging. More nights like this and word would get around with who knows, some more activity spreading to the earlier days.

The evening drew to a close at a realistic time. The final customers had left by 11.50pm enabling me to close up and complete the wind down shortly after midnight. I was relieved as the following day was most definitely going to be hectic.

One week had elapsed since taking over the pub and things were certainly moving quickly. I was up early and had received the frozen food delivery before 9.00am. I went about the bar preparations like a man possessed. I had a little 'fun' time in the process as well. Our log stock was running low so out the tractor and trailer came and two full trailer loads were collected from the log store and transported to the respective bar fireplaces. The task was so much easier to complete than before with the aid of my new toy. Before putting the tractor mower away I quickly mowed the village green areas with a first season cut. It made all the difference to the look of the immediate area. I completed by mowing the traffic island as well to finish the job. The whole operation only took 40 minutes. It was an undertaking I was happy to continue with as my contribution to keeping the hamlet tidy. I was subsequently thanked for my efforts by the local parish council.

11.30am and the trestle bench delivery arrived as arranged. Malcolm came with one of the other dungaree clad men I had seen earlier in Hothfield. It was a surprisingly large load. I parked up the tractor mower and went to help with the offloading. As I have come to learn it is normally beneficial to offer a tea or coffee on such occasions. Coffee was gratefully accepted and we set about offloading and placing the new garden furniture throughout the beer garden. The three of us got in a good rhythm for the unloading. Malcolm stayed on the lorry and the other guy and I took the benches to their respective locations. It only took about 45 minutes to complete. Sue in the meantime opened the bar on my behalf. The three of us went in and I duly settled up with Malcolm and stood them a drink for their trouble. They were both unaware of the pub's existence. Both were real ale drinkers and after being told about the new introduction of the new ales they were stating they would be returning. They drank up, we shook hands and the two men left. The new benches were a real boon. Everything was coming together nicely.

The lunchtime session passed quickly without incident. We had a small party of ramblers who stayed for lunch. They had enjoyed the service and said they too would be returning in the future.

Lorna popped in with our delivery of eggs, milk and cream. As the Bank Holiday was on us we decided to increase the order in the hope that we were going to be busy. Lorna obliged and went back to her van whilst Sue made her coffee. She was the first to comment on how spick and span everything appeared. The new garden furniture was going to be a boon and the mown pub lawns and village green completed the pleasing picture. She left shortly afterwards to be followed by Stan the soft drinks man. He quickly assessed the stock and gleaned an idea of how busy we had been. 'Not bad at all!' he mused. 'Busier than the other pubs, that's for sure.' he continued. Stan recalculated our usage and adjusted for the oncoming busy weekend and bank holiday. I agreed his figures and left him to restock from his lorry. He had a quick cup of tea on the run and was completed and away within half an hour of arriving. He had a large round to get round so his timing was of the essence.

I spent an hour or so outside fixing some new signs to the pub walls supplied the day previously by Phillip. They indicated the stock availability of the new real ales.

I left them covered until the dray had been the following day. I then went back inside and piped up the remaining two real ale hand pumps in the bar. They just fitted alongside the existing pressure keg beer fonts at both ends of the bar. All I needed now was the beer delivery.

The evening session started quite early. One of the students from up the road was celebrating her 21st. birthday. All four students came in with about a further twenty from the college in Wye. It was a good natured event and good for business. Unlike the earlier student visitation they were intent on having a good time and were happy to pay accordingly. Not only were they drinking, for the first time Sue was put under real pressure in the kitchen as a result of the number of food orders that had been placed. Several locals joined the party throughout the evening as well. It all concluded nicely at 11.30pm and everyone left in high spirits. I cashed up, wound everything down and got to bed at 12.15am. Tomorrow was going to be really hectic as well.

Friday started early. The door bell was rung at 7.15am as the bulk Calor gas delivery vehicle turned up to top up our tank. We were well off the beaten track for a mains gas supply so the bottled alternative was the only solution. The driver gratefully accepted a mug of tea. He had already made three other calls in the area. Being so early no-one was up to offer him the courtesy. He returned the mug rewound the delivery hose and was away within twenty minutes of arriving.

My two daughters and I enjoyed a bacon and egg breakfast together before they left to go to school next door. Sue lay in after her unexpected efforts from the night before. She had deserved it. The girls were made aware of the imminent arrival of Roscoe by their mother the night before. Understandably, they were very excited and would have preferred to have stayed at home. We were both adamant that they should however go to school.

Fortified by my breakfast, I set about the cleaning and bar preparation work. I decided that I would switch the pipe cleaning operation to Friday from Saturday. It seemed better to do it that way as the beer needed to be at its best for the busier weekend sessions, Friday included.

It was an extra operation to somehow fit in but I concluded necessary all the same. Friday was also the re-order day for our frozen food supplier and Phoenix brewery for delivery the following Monday. With it being a bank holiday the delivery day was put back to the Tuesday. I checked our stock level and was concerned to note we only had one spare Fosters lager keg. We had other lagers to fall back on but first choice should be available at all times. Sue was destined to visit the Cash and Carry later. Conveniently, our new spirit wholesaler's depot was next door. I rang them and discovered they carried Fosters as a stock item so Sue could collect a couple of kegs at the same time.

Sue had made an earlier appearance and was getting prepared in the kitchen. I was just in the latter stages of completing the pipe cleaning operation when the door bell rang again for the second time that morning. I went to answer to find Colin and Suzanne at the door. Roscoe was with them but still in the back of their dog carrier vehicle.

Colin in his inimitable style joked 'Here we come, ready or not!'
'Come on in!' I welcomed them both. 'Sue! Colin and Suzanne are here!'
In no time Sue had joined us. We were just as excited at meeting the new arrival.
Suzanne calmly explained that Roscoe would probably take a little time to settle down and should be kept an eye on. She went on that the countryside was probably unknown to him and care should be taken when out walking to avoid upsetting livestock and the like.
All we could hear was the occasional deep throated 'Woof!' from the back of the vehicle. Roscoe was keen to see his new abode and meet his new owners.
Colin went on to say 'Remember, he's a big dog. You must show him whose boss. Be strict and firm. He'll take the slightest liberty!'
We all went out to the rear of the parked vehicle. There he was in all his splendour!
He sported a jet black, long haired glistening fur coat with a white chest, one white paw and a white tip to his tail. It was almost as if someone had dipped his tail in a pot of emulsion. His head was massive in relation to the size of his body. It was out of proportion due to being unloved and under fed for so long. It did not matter to us – our first impressions were 'here's our boy!'
Suzanne let Roscoe out of the van on his lead. Almost maternally she was telling the dog how he must be a good boy.
He was a big animal even now, but the scars of his previous bad experiences were all to plain to see. I knelt down to welcome him. Sue shed a tear and the lead was handed over. Roscoe had arrived!
We all filed into the pub with Roscoe. He was immediately let off the lead to investigate his new surrounding. Newfoundland's are normally out door animals by choice. It was never our intention to have him inside unless by choice on his part if the weather was too cold or inclement. He had his 'kennel' retreat shared with the rear beer store should he need shelter from the elements. His duties would be to guard the beer stock as well so we thought. There was also a large lean-to for storing empty kegs and beer crates that Roscoe could stay under if he preferred.
He settled very quickly having investigated the bar areas, restaurant, rear stores and corridors and was looking to check outside. The rear garden was totally fenced so I let him out; leaving the back door open should he want to come back in.

Whilst in the garden Roscoe had his first encounter with Basil. The former animal was not amused to find another canine inhabitant sharing his domain again. He sat on the edge of the beer store roof close to the edge in full view of Roscoe and waved his tail tantalizingly just out of reach of the dog. Roscoe was up on his hind legs, jumping and barking at the cat in an effort to catch its swishing tail. Every so often the cat would hiss and spit at the dog directly to let him know who was boss. I think Roscoe probably thought much the same, that he was boss and the cat should be kept on the roof and out of the way! This performance was going to be repeated many, many more times in the future but always ending in stalemate as boredom or something else became more interesting.

We opened up and had a celebratory drink with Colin and Suzanne. I offered to pay for any treatment or cost that had been incurred with our new boy. Colin explained the Newfoundland Society had met all the expenses. I therefore gave them £100 as a donation to the Society funds. Suzanne explained it was not necessary but we both felt it was a small price to pay for bringing our new boy into the family.

They both left shortly afterwards leaving us with strict instructions on feeding and disciplining.

Roscoe had to embark on a highly nutritious diet to remedy the chronic loss of bodyweight he had experienced but without being over fed.

As they were leaving an Age Concern minibus arrived in the car park. The driver asked if we were open and if so, could we provide lunches for the fifteen members in his bus. It was nice to have the old dears in for lunch. We opened the restaurant for them which they very much appreciated. They loved the old pub and its character and surprised both Sue and myself at how much they ate and more surprisingly drank!

It was a very nice start to the lunchtime session.

Other customers were appearing from all points of the compass. Our earlier week's reputation was spreading and punters were taking time to come and find us. If this was anything to go by, we should be in for good trading throughout the May Day Bank Holiday weekend. Sue had the benefit of the kitchen looking directly out over the private garden. She could keep an eye on Roscoe and any of his antics. He was settling down nicely. He had visited all the corners, marked, scented, sniffed and checked out his new domain.

The patio area directly outside the kitchen was ideal. He was tall enough, when stood on his hind legs, to look directly into the kitchen and watch what was going on inside. The occasional bark would be made to remind the occupants of his presence and 'beg' for a snack or two. The sight of his massive, expectant head in the window was difficult to ignore, so from a very early time Roscoe was being spoilt rotten by all of us.

The session came to an end and the pub was cleared by 3.00pm just in time for the West Country Products dray to arrive. The driver had a deuce of a job finding the pub and so was most apologetic for her late arrival. In fact it was just as well she was late as both Sue and I were totally committed to the hilt, during the earlier session.

Bobby, the dray woman and driver I believe was pretty unique. An ex-Army Military Police woman had taken on her new role as one of few women dray operators. It is true to say dray work is very much a male dominated 'profession'. Good physique and strength are but two of the requirements to be a successful dray person. Bobby was not unattractive but certainly not to be crossed either.

Each full cask of 72 pints would weigh 100+ pounds in weight and need to be manhandled in and out of the cellar. The awkward shape and fluid content would make the kegs even more difficult to contend with. Bobby and I set about unloading as quickly as possible. She showed no signs of difficulty whatsoever. Her heavily tattooed massive biceps put mine to shame. The twelve casks didn't take long to offload and empties put back on the dray. Phillip had come up trumps again. Bobby also gave me a dozen 'freebie' garden umbrellas from various brewers to adorn our new trestle tables and truly complete the newly made over beer garden.

Previous customs prevailed when I invited Bobby in for a drink and to meet the other half. Sue liked Bobby. Niceties completed and expecting her to have a coke or a fruit juice, she eyed up the beer pumps and asked for a pint of Ruddles, one of our premium real ales. The dog was barking in the back garden. Bobby asked what kind of a dog it was. I explained it was a 'Newfee'. She was a dog lover and had been involved with handling Alsatians when she was an MP. She knew what a 'Newfee' was and asked to see the dog. I opened the back door and let Roscoe in. He bounded round to the bar to be made a fuss of. Bobby loved him, but as time was pressing the fussing ended prematurely. She downed her pint and left after I had signed for the delivery. Next time there should be more time to chat and play with Roscoe further.

I quickly returned outside with Roscoe in tow. I manhandled the first of the new casks into the cellar, much to Roscoe's delight! What a great game he thought. Barking and snapping all around the barrel as it was moved. As I started the cellar reorganisation I realised two empty casks had been left behind. As they were empty I could easily lift them up and carry them outside. At that point I noticed Roscoe didn't want to play. I rolled the empty barrel along the path to the empty storage area. The dog couldn't have cared a less. However, the minute I went for a second full new barrel – look out!

Roscoe was straight at it. It was exactly the same reaction from the dog as before. He was excited, barking and snapping at the barrel as it was rolled along the ground. Care had to be exercised to avoid being bitten. What a strange reaction I thought. Full barrels, Roscoe went berserk, empty barrels he couldn't give a fig! I tested this theory again and on all counts it was the same outcome. I called Sue to come and watch. It was exactly the same. Totally inadvertently we had discovered our own unofficial 'beer minder' and alarm system combined in one. In such a short time Roscoe was proving his worth to us.

Shortly afterwards the girls came home from school. They met Roscoe for the first time and were all over him. Vice a versa Roscoe seemed to bond immediately with both girls. We decided to take him for his first 'walkies' together. We shut up shop and all five of us went off down the lane past the side of the pub. Roscoe was bright-eyed, bushy tailed all the way. He was extremely good on the lead. We all took it in turns to walk him until we reached one of Jim Peterson's field's that was empty of stock to let Roscoe run free. He loved it. At first he wasn't sure but soon realised that he was with us to stay. He bounded around us all like there was no tomorrow. He even returned when called. What a dog we all thought. The girls thought of him as the brother they never had! Roscoe had been officially welcomed to our family.

He was truly in doggie heaven now.

CHAPTER 6 – Up and Running

Martin appeared for the Friday evening session as arranged at 6.00pm. I took the opportunity to show him the general workings of the bar and cellar. Clearly his experience was very limited probably confined to dealing with the punters only.

I took the opportunity to check the two real ale additions that had been delivered by Bobby earlier in the day. Unfortunately the Harveys Sussex Bitter was still a little cloudy and would not be available until the following day. The Fullers London Pride was fine and could be served immediately. Both beers were advertised on the external signage and beer mats laid out on the tables.

Sara turned up for work at 6.30pm and prepared the restaurant before assisting Sue in the kitchen with garnishes and the like. The Dew Drop machine was coming alive.

I checked on Roscoe and gave him his evening meal that had been prepared earlier. Needless to say it didn't take long for him to consume it and lick his bowl clean. He seemed very happy and contented with his new surroundings. Both girls decided to play with the dog outside in the back garden. Basil just watched on from his vantage point on the beer store roof.

Right on 7 o'clock the doors were opened and we were ready for business.

Our first arrivals turned up shortly after 7.15pm. A foursome from Wye who explained they were former customers of the pub under Geoff's regime. I served them and took them on face value, standing the first round of drinks on the house as it was their first returning visit. They appreciated the gesture and remarked upon the changes that had been made in the bar. I asked if they were dining, and if so, directed them to the restaurant to observe the other changes that had been made. Clearly the lounge area was most welcome as they took their choice of seat. Sara offered them menus for their selection from the bar meals on offer.

In the meantime other customers appeared, fast and furious.

Mike and Janet made their first visit. They were our next door neighbour on the other side living in the School House. Janet was the final Rose family member to visit and was the caretaker of the school. Mike worked in Ashford for a distribution company.

I served them with their initial drinks on the house and introduced myself to them. They were not major users of the pub as we were to find out. Their son, David however was, and could be a bit of a handful on occasions. Uncles Tom and Rod were seen on various occasions keeping young nephew David on the straight and narrow! Martin in the meantime seemed to be settling down quite well. He had a pleasant and polite way of dealing with the punters and with practice was getting quicker at serving.

By 8.00pm the restaurant was well over half full. Both the girls were performing well although the volume of orders coming in meant a slowing up of service was inevitable. The bar remained busy which was a problem. I thought I might be able to slip away and assist in the kitchen. The level of trade in the bar obviously prohibited that option. Extra kitchen assistance would be the only option.

By fluke Terry and Molly came in for their normal Friday night out. I struck immediately and offered Molly a trial part-time position in the kitchen. She was delighted to accept and agreed to start the following lunchtime session. Further shifts would be discussed later as appropriate. The extra money would obviously be useful.

The pub was getting busier all the time. All the Friday night regulars were in along with a host of visitors from other areas. The restaurant was full to brimming and we were obviously in for our best session since arriving at the pub. The real ales were doing very well albeit there were a lot of customers disappointed that the Harveys ale was not ready. The remaining three real ales probably benefited as a result. Martin and I were kept very busy right up to closing time. We called last orders at 11.00pm and only observed people starting to leave shortly before 11.30pm. Sara and Sue had done well and had completed the shutdown procedures in the kitchen by 10.45pm. This gave them the opportunity for the girls to relax and wind down, socialising in the bar. It was good to see the landlady out front with the punters. A lot had been happening in the last few days and it was the ideal opportunity to spread the word of our new family member as well. By midnight the bar was left with immediate locals only and most of them were getting ready to leave. Sue and I were very pleased with both Martin and Sara's contribution. It was clear that extra support, particularly in the kitchen would still be needed.

I broke the news to Sue that I had given Molly a trial part-time position in the kitchen, starting the following day. She was relieved at the prospect of additional catering support in the kitchen. We all enjoyed a last round of drinks prior to finishing the wind down operations. Somehow, it seemed the running of the pub was getting a little easier.

The following morning we were all up early. The girls were already out in the garden playing with Roscoe when we got downstairs. The dog loved every second of their interaction. Basil for his part was still overlooking the proceedings from his safe vantage point. Obviously the new family introduction was being treated with scorn. Suddenly the cat's popularity rating with the girls had taken a tumble.

Sue intended leaving early for the Cash and Carry and Spirit Wholesaler visit that was postponed from the day earlier due to the arrival of Roscoe. After such a busy previous night we really were well down on Fosters lager and Vodka stock. Both had taken a bit of a hammering. Sue knew what was required in the kitchen and left immediately after a breakfast of coffee and toast. She needed to get back as quickly as possible with Molly due to start work that day. For my part I got on with the normal daily cleaning and bar preparation routine. Thank goodness the 'pipes' were cleaned the day earlier. Amanda, our eldest daughter came in to ask if they could walk Roscoe. After yesterday's good performance I agreed that both girls could take the dog on the same route as yesterday. She was told that under no circumstances should the dog be taken in the field if any animals had been moved there.

I watched from the kitchen window as the three of them took off down the rear lane. They all appeared to be having good fun and were inseparable so it seemed. A good bonding exercise was taking place under my very eyes.

I was just completing the final cleaning procedures an hour or so later when Sue returned from her mission. She came in a little agitated having seen the girls in the field down the lane playing with Roscoe. I showed little concern explaining that I felt it was important they should bond quickly with the dog. I was happy they were responsible enough to look after Roscoe, just as I felt, given time, Roscoe would look out for the girls as well. We unpacked the food from the car and the two kegs of Fosters, one of which I took straight in to the cellar. Time was pushing on as Sara, Martin and Molly arrived for their shifts.

Being the eternal optimist I suggested to Sue that perhaps we could try an all-day breakfast on the specials board. We had everything in stock and this variant seemed to becoming quite popular in other establishments. Sue agreed to give it a go so it was chalked on the daily special board at £3.50. It was a little more expensive than other similar meals but I felt the premium price was justified.

Sue spent a little time with Molly explaining the kitchen operation whilst Sara readied the restaurant. Martin completed the finer points of bar readiness as I took a quick shower and change before opening up.

As I was rushing I noted the return of the girls and Roscoe. They had been away for about an hour and enjoyed every minute of it. Roscoe made a beeline for the kitchen window, jumped up and gave a quick attention seeking bark. Sue obliged with a couple of treat Bonio's she had just purchased from the Cash and Carry. The dog woofed those down like no tomorrow. I returned to the bar to check all was in order with Martin. I made a final check and went to open up.

We had been blessed with a dry day of hazy sunshine and quite warm for the time of year. It was a little early at 11.45am but the car park was already filling up with customers. All the signs indicated we would continue where we left off the night before. I returned behind the bar. Martin was already serving when I remembered I had to draw off the real ales, particularly the Harveys to ensure they were up to scratch. The Harveys had cleared overnight and tasted divine. The other three ales were fine as well. It was strange to note that not one customer so far was a local or regular. We were both serving as fast as possible. Harveys was going like wild fire.

A few customers decided to use the newly furnished beer garden. I opened the lower bar door for ease of access for those in the garden. The old place was really coming alive.

Food orders started being taken shortly after noon. The all-day breakfast seemed quite popular as were the range of ploughman's we had on offer. Sara had already put the Cona machine on and fresh bread rolls were baking in the kitchen. The combination of the coffee and bread bake aromas wafted into the restaurant and bar areas. If you weren't hungry when you came in you soon were once the aroma combination struck you!

Everything was fine except that a bottleneck was becoming obvious. Taking food and drink orders at the bar was becoming tedious. Restaurant customers were getting frustrated waiting to be served in the bar. Something needed to be done quickly. I summoned Sara and gave her a cash float from the safe, duplicate order pads and told her to take food orders directly in the restaurant for customers who were seated there. Sara devised a table numbering system to keep track of all the orders. Everything ordered had to be paid for in advance to minimize the risk of 'walkouts'. Sara quickly understood what was required and set up the new cash drawer in the old restaurant bar counter. We would still take food orders for the beer garden at the bar and identify where the customers were sitting. The new system seemed to be working well and food service efficiency was improving. In the meantime Sue and Molly had most things under control. Batches of chips and rolls were being prepared in advance to minimize the overall order turn round cycle.

We were really on song. Customers seemed happy with our offerings and almost all were saying they would return as they left.

Tom and Smurve appeared shortly before 1.00pm. They had both been to work for a morning shift and were surprised at the level of business. They both 'fought' their way to Tom's normal perch position and settled quickly. Martin went to serve them to be met with the tell tale spluttering of the Fosters pump running empty. I was ready this time and quickly went in to the cellar to change the barrel. I was back in a jiffy and told Martin all was well again. A couple of final splutters came from the pump and the amber nectar started to flow again. Tom had received his English Ale in the meantime.

'Bloody 'ell mate! Is it free beer or something?' Tom quizzed me.
'Bank holiday and these new beers just started. That's what's brought them out.' I replied.

Both men undeniably liked a busy pub as I did. However, this busy was another matter.

Tom added to the lovely aromas in the bar by stoking up his pipe. One could almost enjoy standing by him just to smell his pipe smoke.

Outside, parking was becoming an issue. Cars were being parked everywhere. Double parking in some places leaving the smallest of gaps to get through.

The two friends at the bar had concluded that the pub had never been this busy in Geoff's or his predecessor's time.

The last recollection that trade was at this level coincided with a wedding party and barbecue together at the pub.

Even though food was technically stopped at 2.00pm the backlog of orders had built up despite the differing procedures. Between the three of them they had served in excess of 150 bar meals with 12 or so still to complete. When it was possible either of us from the bar had taken through drinks to keep everyone happy. The learning curve was a steep gradient but we had done really well to overcome it. This I knew would be the norm to be expected if, as and when Sunday Roasts were to be offered. Clearly further support would be required if we were to embark on such a venture.

The last food orders were sent out and the kitchen closed. Molly and Sue started to clear away in preparation for the closing procedures which Molly had to be acquainted with. She was a fast learner and generally only had to be shown once. Sara held the restaurant operation together very well under the circumstances. The new ordering system did allow a greater degree of control and was here to stay with a little tweaking in order.

The final customers left by 3.30pm that afternoon. We all assisted in the resetting operation. Glasses and crockery were collected from the garden by our daughters with the result the pub was ready for action again shortly after 4.00pm. The three staff members left, agreeing to return two and a half hours later. Sue and the girls took Roscoe out again, on a different route this time. For my part I cashed up and was delighted at my findings. Even with the extra staff expense we really were well ahead of target. I resurrected Geoff's old till from the under stair store cupboard and set that up for use in the restaurant. This would undoubtedly make life a bit easier for Sara and be more secure in use. Having completed everything I set about making our tea for the family and Roscoe's as well to be taken on their return.

The weather had remained fine all day and into the evening with a stunning sunset to boot. All five of us were ready for the evening challenge ahead and had prepared accordingly. In similar vein to the previous lunchtime session, cars were already filling up the car park. I got Martin to open up a little early at 6.45pm. Ironically the first couple in were Tom and Helen.

'Avoiding the rush mate. Don't want any bugger knickin' my seat!' Tom mumbled. His earlier visit was clearly in mind.

I had already got his English Ale and pot in place as he asked Helen what she wanted to drink. She decided on an orange juice and lemonade which I duly poured for her.

'What's wiv this 'ere Harvey's beer boy?' Tom asked as I pulled the first of two pints for the next customer.

'It's a very popular beer! Nice and smooth. Not over strong either.' I pulled an extra sample glass for Tom and left it for him to try.

I took the two eagerly awaited pints to the waiting customers who duly paid and took their drinks into the beer garden.
Tom tried the beer, said how nice it was but preferred his English Ale.
'Variety's the spice of life old man!' I commented as I took the empty half pint glass away.
Business kept building throughout the early evening. For the first time I switched on the outside floodlights that bathed the beer garden and car park in bright sodium yellow light. It transformed the look and charm of the old building and could be seen from miles around. By 8.30pm every seat in the house was taken, the restaurant was full and the trestle tables outside were all occupied. There was standing room only in the bar and beer was being passed over three people deep waiting to be served. Martin and I were working at full tilt. The three women were likewise totally committed to serving their customers. The atmosphere was absolutely brilliant both inside and outside. Even Roscoe joined in. He stood on hind legs with his front paws between the pales of the fence alongside the beer garden. He loved the attention and no doubt the treats that were obviously being fed to him. He was rapidly becoming a celebrity, particularly with the younger visitors to the pub. I took a second to stand back and take in the ambience. 'This is just how it should be!' I thought to myself. 'Lots of happy people enjoying themselves without a care in the world, that was what being 'mine host' was all about' I mused. The tills were ringing my kind of music as well. What could possibly go wrong?
I was brought back to reality by a request for another round of beer. I took the man's order and went to pull the beer he requested. As I pulled the second pint he requested I looked up to see Basil, the pub cat coming across the car park approaching the open lower saloon bar door.
The floodlighting highlighted everything. Basil was bringing home a prized, newly caught hare in his mouth. He was very proud of himself and obviously wanted to share his 'prize' with all these visitors in our house. I ran cold but had to continue with serving. The cat was within a couple of feet of entering the busy bar with the hare. Enough! I thought and had to act quickly. There wasn't enough time to get out from behind the bar. I did what I felt was the next best thing.

'Basil! Out!' I shouted at the cat, gesticulating with my right arm at the same time and pointing to the car park. The cat stopped, hare in his mouth and stared up at me from the open door. A moment passed and Basil thought better of it to come in so continued his journey across the front of the pub, to scale the roof to the shower room window.

Naturally, after my outburst and for a couple of moments later the pub went silent. You could almost hear a pin drop. A second or two later and everything was back to normal. The general hubbub immediately reinstated itself.

I apologised to my customers for the unexpected delay and finished their order. They seemed to understand. I took their money and turned to the till, rang in the amount, withdrew the change and turned back to hand over the coins.

The customer alongside was a little short, bald-headed man wearing horn rim round spectacles, very much akin to the comedian, Benny Hill's assistant from years gone by. He had returned to the bar with empty glasses in hand.

'Can I get you a refill sir?' I asked.

'No thanks' he replied. 'We're leaving. Had a lovely evening but it's come to an abrupt end. Will we be allowed back?' he concluded

'What the hell's he on about!' went through my mind. Suddenly the penny dropped.

'I'm sorry sir. Is your name Basil by any chance?' I asked

'Yes it is' he replied.

'Were you sitting by the door over there by any chance?' I continued

'The wife and I sat right next to the door' he answered.

I couldn't contain myself any longer and just burst out laughing.

'I'm sorry sir! Basil is the pub cat. He was just about to come in and bring the hare he had just caught! I wasn't speaking to you!' I retorted, still finding the incident funny.

The older gentleman wasn't immediately amused.

'Go on have a drink with me! Let's have no hard feelings, eh?' I offered.

'Oh, go on then. Two halves of Harvey's please.' he requested then burst in to a beaming smile and chuckled quietly to himself.

'Who'd of thought it? Chucked out of the pub for the sake of a cat!' he mused as he left with the recharged glasses.

I concluded the incident by offering a 'thumbs up' to the two of them. They raised their glasses in response. Pride had obviously been reinstated.

With the incident over I got back to the reality of serving again. 'When y'er ready boy!' Tom called expecting a refill. Helen also had a refill. By now the Rose clan had come on in and were huddled around Tom and Helen in the upper saloon bar. Tom duly did the honours completing the round, offering me a drink in the process. I had a half of Harvey's with Tom to show willing.

Everyone seemed very much at ease in the bar. Martin had gone through to check on the girls and their drink requirements. He returned to let me know all was well in the restaurant and the girls were handling the strain admirably.

Throughout that session I believe everyone we had come across during our short occupation of The Dew Drop Inn had visited the pub. With it being a Bank Holiday there was an hour extension to the normal drinking time. It was chilly outside now and a lot of the beer garden customers tried to come inside to the warmer bar. Some hardier types stayed outside. It was still a beautiful clear night. In the years we owned the pub, I don't recall any time busier than this one session.

By the time we closed up and the last customers had left it was shortly after 12.30am.

We five staff members sat in the bar and had a relaxing win down 'staff drink' and chat, musing on the earlier events during the session. The 'Basil incident' took pride of place and amused the girls on hearing it recounted. Molly had fitted in well and alleged she actually 'enjoyed' the mayhem. Martin and Sara had likewise done well and just took everything in their stride. Sue and I were grateful for their support and wondered what it would be like the following day. Molly volunteered her services for Sunday night which we gratefully accepted, just in case it was busy as it was still the bank holiday. All three confirmed they would be happy to work the Monday lunchtime session as well.

I decided we should play safe and took them up on their offer. Monday night though, we would be on our own.

Sue and I eventually got to bed shortly after 1.35am. Bank holidays may be fun but in this line of business they can be exhausting!

Sunday morning had come too soon! It was a brilliant, almost summer type day with small puffy clouds in the sky. In the direct sunshine it was warm and comforting. Obviously it was the warmest day of the year so far. We both struggled to get up but needs must. I slipped on jeans and a tee shirt and headed downstairs. The bar and restaurant areas had been partially sorted out the night before. As it was such a fine day I decided not to light the fires. By not lighting the fires I gave myself the additional task of clearing out all the ash which had accumulated. I went and got the trusted tractor and trailer out for the purpose. Both girls had not seen my new toy. Amanda the eldest daughter was really impressed. Both of them were treated to a ride in the trailer much to Roscoe's displeasure. He was missing out and that was not on. In the end Sue looked out of the upstairs window to see me driving the tractor around the beer garden and car park with Roscoe and the girls sat in the trailer behind. They all loved the experience. The girls finally took Roscoe off for his morning constitutional walk leaving me to continue with my duties, having had my 'mad minutes' of fun with them all. Having sorted the fireplaces I turned my attention to quickly restocking the logs. The two fires burnt a surprisingly large amount of wood when in use. Not lighting the fires would not only be cleaner but would save on the cost of logs. I finished by putting the 'toy' away and went inside to finish the cleaning operation. By the time I had finished the polishing and hoovering through, Roscoe and the girls had returned and were happily playing football in the rear garden.

I had now turned my attention to re-bottling and cellar duties. On checking I noted that two of the real ales were getting low so spiled the replacement casks to let the beer breathe in readiness for dispensing. Spiling allows the pre-conditioning of the beer and is an important operation in real ale husbandry. Keg beers do not require spiling. They are conditioned and filtered at the brewery. I noted one keg bitter was running low as was the AK mild. I removed the Fosters empty keg from the following day and went to the beer store for replacement barrels of the bitter, AK mild and Fosters lager. The dog was totally un-interested in what I was doing.

The minute I started to move the first barrel Roscoe left the football game and became excited as he had done previously a couple of days before. Barking and snapping all the time, it was almost as if he was trying to stop me taking or moving the full barrels away again. I got the first barrel into the cellar, much to Roscoe's disconcertion. I went back for the second. Again just as before the dog went totally berserk as was the case for the third barrel. I concluded it must be something to do with the noise the barrels made when rolled over the concrete. When full the barrel must have a deeper tone differing to that when empty. I finished in the cellar and completed the 'bottling up' in the bar.

The staff support arrived at 11.30am. I left Martin to finish up the bar final preparation and open up enabling me to pop up to shower and change.

Sue in the meantime had put the roast potatoes in the oven and searched the freezers for 'old' stock for the bar 'freebies'. Onion rings and some battered vegetables were duly deep frying, so I thought ready to go on the bar. The first batch of rolls was in the oven to bake. Molly was preparing the cheese on sticks for the bar and salad garnishes for the bar meals. Sara had readied the restaurant and put the coffee on. The coffee and bread aromas started to filter through to the main sales areas as on previous occasions.

I came down to the bar to find the AK gang already in enjoying their first drinks.

Trade was steady so I decided to stay with the customers to socialise for the time being. Jim Peterson surpassed himself and insisted on buying me a pint. I gratefully accepted and enjoyed the 'gang's company. The conversation invariably got round to our new member of the family. Jim was understandably concerned for his livestock with a new dog in the area, particularly one the size of Roscoe. I re-assured him that his concerns would probably be unfounded as I explained Roscoe's awful life history. Jim sympathised and was almost apologetic.

Bob and Sue entered the bar, swiftly followed by Tom. Things were beginning to hot up and business was building.

Bob and Sue had walked up from their bungalow, making the most of the glorious weather. They had met Roscoe as they passed. As was becoming his characteristic pose, Roscoe was on his hind legs, paws between the pales of the chestnut fence around the back garden.

He loved being paid attention to. Bob being a dog lover was only too pleased to oblige. Having made a fuss of Roscoe he came in to the pub.

Seeing I was talking with Jim, Bob made a beeline to join in our conversation. He was most taken with Roscoe. Having now met and vetted the dog, Bob went on to re-assure Jim that Roscoe would not pose a threat to their livestock. Bob was not wrong. Furthermore, he would always find time to stop and make a fuss of Roscoe when he passed down the back lane.

Business was now rapidly building with customers looking to both eat and drink. I thanked Jim and Bob for their support and went behind the bar. I collected the liberally salted 'freebies' from the kitchen and took them with me to place on the bar.

The AK gang members weren't slow at coming forward. The four adults were tucking in to the free offerings on the bar. No-one seemed interested in what they were eating and certainly didn't ask. Ann was the first to comment that the onion rings seemed a bit 'rubbery'!

Secretly I thought to myself 'Bloody cheek. They're free!'

Not satisfied with the first complaint she came back with a second.

'They taste a bit fishy as well as being rubbery?'

My previous thoughts stayed in my mind. 'The front of some people!' I thought.

Only then it crossed my mind to check with the kitchen. I asked Sue about the onion rings she had sent out to the bar.

'You silly old sod! They're not onion rings, they're Calamari rings. Squid. You know!' Sue retorted scornfully.

I chuckled to myself as I went back behind the bar. I couldn't wait to let Ann know what I had discovered!

'Ann!' I attracted her attention. 'What makes you think their onion rings?'

'Well, if their not, what are they?' she replied. The AK gang members momentarily stopped eating to hear my answer.

'They're Calamari rings. Squid. You know!'

Ann was horror struck. 'Squid, those horrible slimy things in the sea?'

'The very same' I replied, handing her a paper serviette.

'Do you not like them, there lovely with tartar sauce you know?'

Ann made a swift exit to the ladies toilet. She returned a little while later.

'No I do not like them. I thought they were onion rings!'

'Best to check next time eh!' Touché I thought to myself.

Funnily enough the next time the 'freebies' were reloaded on the bar half an hour later it was quite noticeable the AK Gang seemed to steer clear of the calamari rings. They stuck rigidly to the potatoes and cheese.

Business remained brisk throughout the lunchtime session. Even with the fine weather we didn't approach the same levels of trade we had experienced the day before.

Tom had a simple explanation for the irregularity

'It's simple boy! Sun comes out like today, everyone buggers off to the beach! Come tonight they all come home and they want beer and food, Seen it so many times.'

Bearing in mind we were only 10 miles from the sea there seemed to be sound thinking behind Tom's theory. If he was right, and being short staffed for the evening shift we were probably going to be up against the wall.

Smurve came into the bar, ordered his usual pint of Fosters and stood a round for the remaining members of the Rose clan present.

He settled the round and in the process offered his excuse for not returning the previous evening.

'I came up 'ere and saw how busy the pub was. I thought yesterday's dinner time had carried on! Too busy for me so I went down to the Five Bells in Brabourne.' he told Tom and me. He continued 'There was reasonable trade down there but nothing like here. Hans was sick as a parrot to hear you were so busy when I told him.'

Smurves last point concerned me. Hans and Pauline ran a very nice business in Brabourne. We had met in the interim period before we took over The Dew Drop Inn. They had only been at the Five Bells a couple of months. Hans must have wondered what was going on himself. We were to become close business allies later on in our respective ownerships but this was early days. Neither of us wanted to out do each other. We both felt there was enough business to go round so we could share equally.

The session concluded slightly better than a normal Sunday lunchtime. Sue wound up the kitchen as normal and released Sara and Molly just before 2.30pm. As we were not over busy I let Martin leave with Sara expressing my thanks to both of them and confirmed the Monday arrangement. The remaining session had been extended to 3.00pm with the extra bank holiday extension. The main rush had been and gone and I was left in the bar with the hardcore customers. I took the opportunity to sound Smurve out if he intended coming up that evening. He said he was so I went straight to the point.

'If Tom is right and we are busy tonight I might be in a little bother. Martin and Sara aren't in. Molly is but I think I might be in trouble running the bar on my own. Who knows?'

'No problem mate! I'll come up, have a couple of drinks and if necessary give you an 'and.' Smurve offered
'Cheers mate. I'll owe you if it happens.'
I refilled Smurve's glass and put an English Ale on the bar for Tom. Helen had left earlier to prepare Tom's lunch. Bob had a refill of his cold Guinness and Sal had a half of lager. The AK Gang had diminished to Jim and his wife. They both gratefully accepted halves of AK mild each.
I took the opportunity to sample the ales to check their suitability. They were all fine.
I popped into the cellar to see how the 'spears' were set. The Harvey's was almost running on fresh air. The Fullers and Ruddles were halfway down. The Burton ale was the least popular beer by consumption and only a third down. Reserve changeover casks were ready as and when. As the Burton ale was lagging on sales I decided to promote it by dropping the price to £1.00 a pint. I had learned that some of our customers drink with their eyes; price is the main consideration. The reduced price I hoped would induce a higher throughput.
I returned to the bar and pulled a full pint of Harvey's for myself hoping it would empty the barrel. The beer tasted fine but experience can tell when the cask content is nearing the end.
The good lady came and joined us in the bar, sporting a large mug of coffee. It was a pleasant winding down to the lunchtime session which concluded by 3.30pm as the last customers left. Having shut up the two of us quickly reset everything ready for the evening session. We were getting quiet masterful of the art of resetting quickly and painlessly. Our tasks were completed by 4.00pm giving us time to walk Roscoe again as a family.
On this occasion we went up through the hamlet towards Hassel Street where there were some woods. The time of year meant primroses would be out and it would be a new experience for the dog. The girls took it in turn to hold the lead. Kate the youngest walked alongside Roscoe and was barely a foot taller. He never once pulled or ran amok in any way.
He really was such a docile, gentle giant of a dog. Once in the woods Roscoe was let off the lead to explore and do his own thing. He loved his individual adventure on his own whilst it lasted. The white tip to his tail always gave his position away. He responded very quickly as and when any of us called him which was another bonus.

We walked in the woods until shortly after 5.00pm and then made our way back to the pub. It was gone 5.30pm by the time we arrived home. We sat down for our tea with the girls shortly before 6.00pm having fed Roscoe previously.

No sooner than we finished Sue and I had to get prepared for the evening session.

Between us we decided that in the absence of Sara, we would revert back to all orders being taken over the main bar. Molly would have to take on part waitressing role whilst Sue would arrange most of the meal preparation.

Molly turned up shortly afterwards and seemed totally happy with the interim arrangements. Only time would tell if it would be a success. Molly put the coffee machine on and started to lay up the tables. Sue readied the kitchen and we were off.

I switched on the bar and festoon lights and on cue slid the bolts on the two doors. Just like the previous night it was a perfect evening. The only difference was there were no customers waiting. It gave me time to check out the Harvey's. I started to pull a pint only to find that just over half full the beer went very cloudy. The end of the cask had come. I ran a jug of water and took it into the cellar, removed the pipe from the spear and put it into the jug of water. I returned to the bar, collecting the slop bucket on the way through and placed it under the beer spout and started to pump the engine. In no time the cloudy pipe content started to clear as the water was pumped through the system. Once the water was completely clear I went back to the cellar, removed the spear from the cask and thoroughly washed it with sterilising solution, rinsing well on completion. The spear was then inserted into the spare cask I had conditioned earlier. The pipe was reconnected to the spear and the liquid pulled through from the bar until the new beer was running clear. I checked the beer for clarity and sampled for taste. Heaven I thought. I returned the slop bucket and jug after emptying and removed the empty cask from the cellar. The last remaining cask of Harvey's was manoeuvred out from the beer store, avoiding the excited dog in the process and placed in the cellar to settle and cool down.

Clive, his son Terry and Phil came into the bar together for their constitutional Sunday night game of darts. I welcomed them and drew their beers as requested leaving them to indulge in their 'arrows'. Smurve was not far behind and took his place at the bar. I pulled him his Fosters as normal. He paid offering me a drink in the process. I accepted a half of the new Harvey's to keep him company. In the meantime all the kitchen preparations were complete and Sue and Molly joined us in the bar as well. Was this the calm before the storm I wondered? Terry was at home at a loose end with the children and had a brainwave. He came over with their two to meet with our girls so they could play together with the dog in the back garden. A cunning plan Terry had figured out that worked, much to Molly's annoyance. Having said that it was a Bank Holiday and Terry felt he deserved his rest and relaxation too!

By now it was 7.30pm and only drinkers were in the bar. I sent out some Cokes and crisps to the children in the back garden. Bob and Tom showed up and joined Terry shortly afterwards. I served the three locals their normal drinks and took their money. Still no food customers appeared. Secretly I thought Tom's earlier theory was wrong. The light was fading outside so I switched on the floodlights, bathing the area in the yellow sodium light. It was almost as if people were waiting for the floodlights as a signal. Cars started to appear from all directions. The serene atmosphere was broken. The two girls went back to the kitchen. Sue contemplated baking some rolls and putting on a couple of batches of chips but held off pending receiving the initial orders.

Tom was absolutely right! The initial surge of our food customers were returning from a trip down to the coast. Ironically, fish and chips were sought after. The all-day breakfast proved to be a close second.

I took the initial order for 6 fish and chip suppers and sent the customers through to the restaurant where Molly was waiting. I took a further order for 3 more fish and chips and 1 Lincolnshire sausage and chips, guiding the customers through to Molly. I rushed the first two orders to the kitchen.

On my return there were more customers waiting.

Instinctively, Smurve knew it was time for him to assist. In no time he was behind the bar. At his request he preferred to serve drinks only, leaving me to take the food orders. It seemed to work quite well. Once the order was taken and paid for customers were sent through to the restaurant. Molly would show them to a table and then come and get the food order to go to the kitchen. This minor deviation from Sara's system worked well when we were operating with just Molly's assistance and was adopted for the future.

Our restaurant had a capacity for 50 permanent covers which could be increased to 62 for special 'banqueting' functions. In the normal configuration we had 12 tables of varying sizes comprising 2, 4 and 6 covers. By 8.15pm all tables were full in the restaurant and late customers elected to eat in the bar if a table was free. Some were just happy to wait until a table came free in the restaurant. We didn't operate a 'table for the night' policy here and customers were encouraged to move to the lounge or bar areas after finishing their meals. Coffee was available in the bar, beer garden and lounge areas to encourage rapid table turnover.

The four of us performed well that evening. At one point I went into the kitchen to assist Sue with the food order backlog. More people were eating than drinking, just as Tom had predicted. Food sales are generally better profit makers so we didn't overly object. All the food preparation continued under the watchful eyes of Roscoe. His face and expectant expression framed by the kitchen window was one of the most endearing memories I have of him to this day. Even though we carried a large stock of frozen food some of the staple items were beginning to show signs of dwindling. Chips in particular had been in high demand as were our jumbo cod portions and both lines beginning to run out. We still had a potentially busy Bank Holiday Monday to get through which concerned me. The end of the food session was welcomed by all of us. The wet sales had kept Smurve busy with steady demand throughout. I left the girls to wind down the kitchen and went back to help Smurve behind the bar.

It was just before 10.00 when I noticed two cars and a white transit van pull into the car park. I couldn't help but notice the B.B.S. Construction Ltd. distinctive signwriting on the side of the van. My old building company! As promised Neil and Grant had got together eleven of my old work colleagues and headed our way for a minor impromptu reunion. Smurve was delighted to meet up with Neil and Grant again.

I was elated they took the trouble to come and see us. It had all the makings of a late night party.

Sue and I finally got to bed shortly before 2.00am. Everyone had a great time. It was a very fitting end to that particular Bank Holiday extended session.

The following morning couldn't have been different. The weather had turned against us. It was miserable with intermittent rain throughout the morning. The pub was set on high ground and was enveloped in low grey cloud. Motivating oneself was made that much harder by virtue of the dismal outlook. Still, hard as it was, the show had to go on. All the normal preparations were concluded as normal. I even backtracked and lit the bar fire again it was that miserable.

Right on cue Martin, Sara and Molly turned up for work. Sue in the meantime had done a quick stock check in the freezers. We were down to our last 2 bags of chips. On average, we had been using 5-6 bags per session over the previous days. Once I was informed of the shortage I thought of a cunning plan. I rang Hans at the Five Bells and asked how well stocked he was with chips. Being a far larger establishment he had far greater stockholding and agreed to let me have a case of 4 bags. I was grateful and said I would pop down shortly to pick them up. I left shortly afterwards and was at the Five Bells within 15 minutes. Hans was waiting for me. They had yet to open. I offered to pay him but he refused. Hans just told me to replace the case when convenient. I was grateful to him and left to return to the pub. Time was getting on and I had left Martin to open up. On my return I noted the weather was just as miserable as when I had left. Who knew what level of trade we could expect?

Having dropped the case of chips off in the kitchen I went upstairs to shower and change. Ten minutes later I returned and entered the bar to find Martin passing the time on the dartboard. No customers as yet. I challenged Martin to a quick game. Unbeknown to me he was a team player and as a result I was completely 'whitewashed'. In the meantime the girls were in the kitchen, relaxing, chatting together drinking coffee.

Our first customers turned up just after 12.30pm. Clive Penn had decided to bring his clan out for a pub lunch.

Clive, his wife, Toby, Charlotte his daughter and her fiancée were in attendance. At least that got the session of too a start. AK mild was the chosen drink all round, pints for the men, halves for the women. They all spied the special all-day breakfast and decided to order for everyone. They were settled in the bar for now. Sara reserved a restaurant table for them.

Jim and Bob came in shortly afterwards. Jim seemed to think the earlier 'onion ring' experience was too much for Ann so she decided to take a raincheck on this occasion.

Smurve, Rod and Tom arrived together with a hardy party of eight walkers.

Martin served the locals as I welcomed the walking party. They were clearly surprised to note the Harvey's on offer with it being a Sussex beer. Six of them went for pints of Harveys', the other two went for Burton at the special price. They were all real ale connoisseurs and were thoroughly enjoying our offerings. They all decided to eat with us as well and checked out the menu. They went through to be met by Sara who pushed two tables together to accommodate the party. After a somewhat shaky start the session was improving and continued to do so through to the end. By the time our 3.00pm closing time came the level of business had recovered quite well. We were ready for a break. The staff were paid and left.

The evening session was to be the unknown quantity.

As happens on so many occasions in our unpredictable climate, the weather played a major part in our final Bank Holiday session. I opened up as normal. The only customers I had before 8.00pm were Colin and Suzanne who paid a courtesy visit to see how Roscoe was settling in.

As it was so quiet I took them both out to the back garden to see for themselves. They were more than happy to see how happy Roscoe was. Sue noted he was obviously putting on weight and he was generally brighter and more alert. Whilst we were there I decided to show them my discovery.

Roscoe had taken up his usual pose on the fence, watching the world go by.

'Watch this' I said to the two onlookers. I went into the beer store and started to roll one of the barrels out towards the rear pub door. The dog immediately went into 'silly mode' as he had done on the previous occasions.

I kept my hands clear of all the snarling and snapping whilst the dog re-enacted the usual excited performance, barking throughout. I manhandled the barrel into the door and the dog reverted to his normal placid self. Both Colin and Suzanne appeared very worried at what they had just witnessed. For his part Roscoe went and lay down at my side.

'That's a pretty serious behavioural problem.' Suzanne said with deep concern. By Colin's expression I could see he was not overly happy at what he had just seen.

'Now watch' I said as I reached for one of the empty barrels.

As in the past Roscoe just lay there. Not in the slightest bit interested as I rolled the empty barrel around the yard area.

Just to prove the point I asked Colin to choose another empty barrel and roll it around. Roscoe just looked on and didn't budge an inch. I went in to the beer store and started to roll another full barrel around. The dog leapt up and went into 'silly mode' in a flash. He immediately calmed once I stood the barrel on end and came back out of the beer store.
Both onlookers gazed in amazement.
'We've never seen anything like it before! Well I'm blowed!' Colin retorted.
Suzanne fondled the big dogs head amongst mutterings of 'who's a clever boy then?'
Roscoe loved the attention. We went back in to the bar
'Have a drink with me' I offered.
Neither was going to refuse. They kept on trying to explain what they had seen whilst I got their drinks.
'It's uncanny I know. It's almost as if Roscoe has been trained to protect the beer!' I surmised 'He's got a job as well now!'
The couple laughed in unison. They were so happy to see Roscoe so settled in his new home. Colin and Suzanne left shortly afterwards.
Just like the previous night, the three of us sat in the bar chatting. It was deathly quiet. Molly made a somewhat strange request.
'I've never pulled a pint before. Is it easy?'
Sue replied
'No time like the present. It's my round, what would you like my love?' jokingly addressing me.
'I'll have a pint of Burton as your buying!' I replied.
'Off you go Molly! I'll have a small lager as well!' Sue instructed Molly.
Molly went behind the bar and under instruction and Sue's watchful eye she pulled her first pint, not badly at that either. Sue then instructed her how to pour her lager.
'There you go. It's as easy as pie!' Sue concluded.
Molly blushed.
'Get yourself a drink.' I told her before leaving the bar. Molly pulled a second small lager for herself just as Smurve came in.
'Bloody hell! Someone's pushed the fire alarm!' he joked seeing the empty pub.
'Fosters for Smurve please Molly while your there.' Sue asked.
Molly poured the pint of lager without any problem.

'That's with me, Molly' I said. Molly duly obliged and returned to the customer side of the bar.

'Cheers mate!' Smurve picked up his beer and had a big draw on the contents.

'Poxy weather!' he snorted 'Hans is dead quiet too. Empty!' he continued.

Smurve passed the Five Bells on his way from Smeeth.

Unbeknown to us, the cosy little chat the four of us were having was going to be a regular event in the future. Both Molly and Smurve were to play a far bigger role in The Dew Drop Inn in the future.

Syd popped up later in the evening alone. Having ordered his first beer he settled down to discuss his proposal. He had given some thought to our earlier discussions and thought my girdle idea was a clever solution to the problem of the splitting column. His idea for the wrought iron scrolled screen was brilliant. He had sketched an idea of a two-handed saw outline being incorporated into the design, emphasising the heritage of the pub. We loved the idea and accepted it out of hand. Syd was duly instructed to go ahead with making the screen and fitting the repair girdles as soon as possible.

Rod appeared later in the bar along with a party of four un-related customers. Smurve had missed his presence the night before and chastised him accordingly for missing 'parade attendance'! He ordered a pint of bitter that Smurve duly paid for, along with beers in the 'wood' for himself and Syd.

The party of four asked if food was available. Molly duly obliged with menus and took their order. On this occasion the party were going the whole hog. Soup starters, main courses, desserts and coffee to follow were all ordered. Molly was happy to handle all the cooking and waitressing giving Sue a well earned rest.

Discovering we were still doing food Rod ordered fish and chips. He was feeling pretty hungry as he had been doing a bit of fencing private work on the side that day and hadn't been home, let alone eaten. He added extra chips and bread and butter to make a chip buttie. This boy was hungry!

Brothers Tom and Bob with Jack and Christina came over a little later and joined the gathering. It was after 9.30pm and looking very much as if the extra hour extended drinking time would not be worth staying open for. Sue and I were feeling the strain of the past Bank Holiday marathon and were completely happy to shut up as normal.

The restaurant party of four finished up and left happy and satisfied shortly after 10.00pm. They said they would return. Molly even received a £2.00 tip for the service she provided. She had been doing the kitchen shutdown procedure whilst waiting for the party to leave. She left shortly afterwards, collecting her wages on the way out.
The pub finally cleared of all customers just before 11.00pm. Tomorrow was the start of another working week albeit shortened by a day. Sue assisted me in the bar closedown enabling us to retire by midnight.

CHAPTER 7 – Reality kicks in

With the recent experiences of our successful bank holiday trade rapidly becoming history our lives at The Dew Drop Inn were beginning to normalise and fit into a set routine. We were no longer 'novelties' in the pub and dare I say it, appeared to have become accepted by the majority of local and regular customers alike. Our girls had adjusted to country life very well and made new friends very quickly. Our style of running the pub was beginning to show through. Whilst not universally popular, our policy of not allowing regular, illicit late night drinking appeared to have become generally accepted. The regular exploiters of Geoff's previous policy were long gone. The local hamlet residents and our immediate neighbours were happier that the previous late night interruptions were a lot less frequent.

The following weeks came and passed without serious incident. My endeavours and efforts to introduce Sunday lunches by the Spring Bank Holiday had foundered. We were mindful of our catering in-experience and preferred to hold off and get things right, rather than prematurely make the quantum leap and get things wrong. A lot of truth in the old saying 'You can't hurry a Murray!'

Our small team was gaining experience all the time. Molly had become a cornerstone of support by working lunchtime sessions on every day except Saturday. She also worked Saturday evenings as well on a regular basis. This meant that Sue and I were only on our own, unsupported for Monday to Thursday evenings. The level of trade at these times could be very erratic and unpredictable. We just took it in our stride and somehow coped. Smurve would be around most evenings and was always happy to assist when the level of trade appeared to be getting out of hand.

Martin and Sara's support played a major support role over the weekend sessions for the time being.

Roscoe in the meantime had totally settled and wormed his way firmly into our lives. He was back to full size and was now a magnificent example of his breed. He liked to show off as well. Banking trips into town were now only able to be carried out with Roscoe in attendance. He was now a regular sight on Monday afternoon's in Wye, sat majestically in the back of our Range Rover with his head out of the real tailgate. He was always happy to accept all the fussing passers by would give him.

Late spring was with us and required a minor tweak to the weekly routine. Grass growth was now at full speed in the gardens and village green areas. As anticipated mowing had become a twice weekly occurrence. The tractor mower made the task easy and bizarrely enjoyable in the fresh country air on Tuesday and Saturday morning before opening the pub. Roscoe would be let out of the rear garden by me whilst I ran the tractor about. It gave him the opportunity to lope around at his leisure investigating all the new sniffs and areas of interest without a care in the world. The only time his attention was disturbed would coincide with a passing large vehicle. We had a twice daily coach service passing through the hamlet that would drop off at the village green. This was the most common cause of disturbance or alternatively Bob's regular passing in his big Claas tractor. Both drivers were aware of the dog presence and were vigilant when he was out. Roscoe would in turn 'see them off' agitated in a similar fashion to that displayed when a full barrel of beer was moved.

Heartbreaking as it was, after leaving the pub some years later, this strange penchant for 'seeing off' large vehicles was Roscoe's downfall when he was accidentally run over by a devastated coach driver. His injuries were fatal and so had to be finally put to sleep. In the meantime we had observed that Roscoe was showing signs of sexual frustration. This normally manifested itself when he would be otherwise engaged playing with the girls or when another dog was nearby that he came in contact with.

I was more than concerned on one occasion watching the three of them playing football in the back garden. Amanda the eldest and tallest daughter seemed to be attracted to Roscoe in the rough and tumble of the game. On a couple of occasions Roscoe tried to mount and 'hump' Amanda. I was incensed and went downstairs to separate the dog and sort out the situation. This situation was repeated again with Amanda so I was told on various other occasions. Surprisingly, it didn't happen to Kate. She always inexplicably seemed to have far more control and bonding with the dog. I rang Mike Potter to discuss this new problem. He had suggested neutering was an option although large breeds of dogs don't take too kindly to losing their 'bits' he advised. Roscoe had had enough traumas in his life so we decided to leave him intact and try to manage the situation.

A rolled up newspaper with rubber bands was what Mike Potter suggested. As and when Roscoe got 'fruity' a swift whack on the snout was probably enough to stop him. It made more noise than actually hurt the dog. Associating his actions with the short, sharp treatment over time, should condition him out of his bad habit. As far as the girls were concerned I was never aware of any other re-occurrences. I wish I could say the same for other residents in the hamlet.

Being so remote, Bodsham Green residents were treated to a fortnightly visit by the Mobile Library Service operated by Kent County Council. The visiting lorry and two librarians would bring a vast array of books for people to browse and take out on loan, once they had been formally registered with the Kent Library Service. Every other Tuesday, the mobile lorry would turn up and park on the village green for a couple of hours for residents to take out and return their borrowed reading matter. It was a service that Sue used more than me. I found I had little time on my hands for reading. There always seemed to be something to keep me occupied. Some of the older residents used the service, some more than others. Mrs. Rose could normally be counted on to visit every time the mobile library visited.

One such nightmarish occasion arose that I recall. It was the Tuesday morning and I had not long started the regular first mowing session of the week. I was on the tractor as normal and all gates were open for access to all areas. As normal Roscoe was unleashed and free to go out and about as he had become accustomed to. He didn't have a care in the world.

Shortly after 10.30am the mobile lorry turned up and parked on the village green right outside the pub. Nothing seemed out of the ordinary in any way. Mrs. Rose came across, offering normal courtesies of the day and climbed the steps into the library. I acknowledged her as I passed on the mower. I continued with the job in hand noticing Roscoe heading across the pub frontage to explore the lane that went down the side of the pub towards Little Holt Farm. There was nothing out of the ordinary so far.

There were a series of farm buildings on the corner of the back lane opposite the pub and bounded by the village green which were part and parcel of Jim's farm. The other side of the farm buildings was the converted former dairy building that was now the student hall of residence.

There was access between and around all the buildings. Molly's and our own children on many occasions used to play hide and seek around this complex.

Mrs. Rose came out of the van and went back home having made her new selection of the next fortnight's reading material. Sue had popped in and similarly returned her book and those the girls had on loan.

By now I was nearing the end of the beer garden mowing, having completed the private rear garden earlier. I wondered where Roscoe was, but was not concerned about him. He wouldn't be far away.

I was just making the final passes and saw another of our elderly hamlet residents walking down the road to visit the mobile library. Arthur and Yvonne Herbert lived in their small detached character cottage just beyond the hall of residence and opposite the telephone box. They were in their dotage years and were a very clean living couple rarely seen out and about in the hamlet. They never frequented the pub. They were both pro-active lay Methodist preachers and naturally would never consider entering our 'house of evils!' We had spoken in the past and were used to exchanging niceties. They were both very grateful to me for my ongoing mowing of the village green including the area directly bordering their dwelling. They kept geese and a few chickens. I believe the purpose was for personal security. To go anywhere near their garden would result in an amazing cacophony of spitting and squawking, second to none. Yvonne was a small, upright woman plainly dressed in grey skirt and jacket and wore a typical Miss Marple style hat from earlier years. She could have so easily been cast for the part. She carried her books in a platen-like pose created by her upturned hands locked in front of her. She was bustling along past the farm buildings.

Horror-struck I watched the scene unfold in front of my very eyes. Roscoe had a cunning plan it seemed. He sneaked unseen through the farm buildings complex and back to the road via the hall of residence. He had seen Yvonne heading towards the mobile library. He must have fancied her, or worse, was deeply in love! He took his chance and mounted her. Yvonne tried desperately in vain to avoid Roscoe's carnal advances. She was faced with the choice of having to hold on to her books and persevere with Roscoe having his 'wicked way', or, dropping the books and fending off our rampant dog. From what I could see the earlier option had been decided upon.

I stopped and leapt off the mower and headed as fast as possible towards Yvonne. Roscoe had locked his front paws around her and was intent on 'going all the way!' I arrived there shortly afterwards and grabbed him by the scruff of the neck and pulled him off the unfortunate Yvonne, who in fairness retained her composure and more importantly her books intact throughout the ordeal. Roscoe shook himself loose from my grasp and realising he was in trouble, took off back to the sanctity of the farm buildings, tail riding high! Yvonne had managed to ignore my bad language directed at the dog during the incident. I offered my profuse apologies for the dog's previous indiscretion. She wasn't amused, making comments along the lines of 'lack of control, shouldn't be allowed and castration should be performed'. My apology was duly accepted allowing her to continue to the library. In the meantime I couldn't see Roscoe anywhere and decided to go back to the mowing.

As time was pushing on, I embarked immediately on to mowing the Village Green. I was mindful that Roscoe was still out on the prowl and tried to be more vigilant in the process. I started with the smaller island and moved on to the longer stretch of green going down just beyond the telephone box and Arthur and Yvonne's cottage. The previous incident was unfortunate for Yvonne but quite comical for any onlooker. Her dogged resistance to keep her books intact was most commendable.

Intently continuing with the job in hand I soon noted Yvonne had left the library and was returning home. Like before, she was holding her new book selection in much the same way and was clearly intent on getting back home. You can probably imagine my reaction as she had just passed the farm buildings as Roscoe leapt out of the entrance to the student's hall of residence and tried it on again with poor old Yvonne. Fortunately, this time I was nearer and responded quickly as my 'dirty old dog' tried to finish where he had failed previously! This time I managed to grab hold of his choke chain collar and wrestled him off the poor little old lady. Twice in one day was clearly most unfortunate. Again I had to offer my sincere apologies to Yvonne who was less forgiving on this occasion. Roscoe felt little in the way of remorse. He seemed to like Yvonne and that was that! I offered every excuse I could and assurances it would never happen again, even though I clearly couldn't guarantee it. Her Christian principles overrode and the dog was duly reprieved and forgiven. Despite the incessant gaggling from the protective geese Yvonne made her way back into the safety of her cottage. I took the dog back and shut him in the rear garden to cool off. Despite my harsh words I still found the incident funny and returned to finish the mowing! Roscoe would obviously need far closer supervision when future visits of the mobile library were being made!

Our ongoing commitments to the business requirements were becoming a lot clearer and onerous as time passed by. It was a difficult balancing act to keep up. Running a pub requires stamina and puts strains on relationships that on occasions can be hard to conceal from the punters. We were no different to any other landlords. Arguments would be commonplace over the most trivial matters but a common harmony had to be maintained in the face of the punters for the sake of the business. We were both anxious to ensure our differences didn't rebound on the children or that they may suffer in any way either.

Roscoe was one of the common bonds in this respect and undoubtedly was playing a bigger part in our lives. Balancing his needs with those of the family and the business were becoming a little more fraught. On countless occasions it would be Roscoe who would defuse a potentially volatile domestic crisis by performing a spontaneous and unplanned funny act which would be the catalyst to defusing a difficult situation. One such situation I recall involved the love hate relationship with Basil the cat.

Sue and I had a difference of opinion regarding a menu makeover in the kitchen that had led to a domestic row. Neither of us was prepared to compromise and the atmosphere remained tense and icy between us. Molly came to work and got a little caught up in the argument, but did her best to stay neutral. It was hardly the best working environment to be in to say the least. The stand off was unresolved and our differences remained for sorting out later. The following incident unravelled under our very eyes.

Basil had become more tolerant of Roscoe now and on occasions could be seen in the rear garden taunting the dog unmercifully. The rear kitchen door had a cat flap in it which the cat rarely used. In fact it was my intention to remove it and block it up, as the cat was far more inclined to use the upstairs shower room window to get in and out of the house.

The environmental health officer would probably have frowned upon the cat flap as it was directly in the main food preparation area of the kitchen. The external door opened directly on to the patio area within our private garden area.

It was a nice summer's day, Basil was laying on the patio, sunning and preening himself in the beautiful sunshine. He was a very clean cat and appeared to take pride in his presentation. Roscoe was engaged well away from the cat in the corner of the garden. Some sort of pang of devilment afflicted Roscoe. It was time to 'settle scores' with the cat. Roscoe watched the cat intently and waited for his chance. Whilst Basil was sat cleaning himself looking away from the dog, Roscoe decided to strike. He took off as fast as his legs allowed him, accelerating all the time towards the cat.

In total silence Roscoe was up to speed and reached the edge of the patio when Basil realised the imminent danger. The cat panicked, it was in a hopeless situation and took the only evasive action it could. It leapt in desperation at the cat flap and thankfully it opened, allowing the relieved animal into the kitchen. Roscoe on the other hand saw his prey quickly disappear and had to take evasive action. The speed he achieved was amazing; his braking was not so good! With little option available to the hurtling dog, he just went head down, nose first at the cat flap. The collision that followed was not as you would expect. No bone crunching, yelping or breaking glass. Just a resounding thud and a clatter as the cat flap was instantly demolished. Roscoe was left with his head totally through the door, the remains of the plastic cat flap strewn over the kitchen floor. The dog had all the looks about him that he had seen stars! 'Shucks! Lost again' seemed to be right across Roscoe's facial expression. The dog had hit the door with so much force that his head and profusion of mane hair had come inside. Trying to get out was another issue. Poor old Roscoe was truly stuck. Basil for his part nonchalantly walked back to the damaged door and swiped Roscoe across his nose with both front paws as penance for the dog's earlier indiscretion. We all burst into laughter defusing the difficult situation that until then had prevailed. Seeing Roscoe's plight I went over and put my foot firmly on his forehead, offered advice along the lines 'This is going to hurt you more than me!' and gradually increased the pressure to release the dog's head. Seconds later Roscoe was free, shook his head and probably vowing to get Basil another day. I found a piece of plywood in the garage and did what should have been done earlier,

blocked up the cat flap permanently. Basil learned something from the experience as well. He was never seen in the garden with the dog again!
Ironically, the matter of the menu makeover was un-resolved and became insignificant as other issues became more pressing to resolve.

CHAPTER 8 – On the crest of a wave

We had been living in our new country environment now for well over three months and had time for the full impact of the change in lifestyle to sink in. I believe it would be fair to say it had most certainly been a bit of a roller coaster ride. Overall it had been considered to have been more of a success than a failure. We were now well into the summer season with long and light evenings and the occasional sultry weather spell was generally uplifting. Harvest season was just around the corner which gave the opportunity for working longer hours and earning more money on the farms. The student fraternity had in the main completed their exams and ended the college term. Most had left with their degree qualifications, a few were resigned to return in the next academic year having failed some of the course they were following. The four students in the hamlet were all successful at achieving high degree qualifications. They hadn't left but decided to remain in residence and work with Jim and Bob on the farm during the harvest season. They felt somewhat obliged to assist having had the previous year's usage of Jim's hall of residence. Jim was not a 'skinflint' farmer and was well known for his higher rates of pay. The students were earning a proper living for probably the first time and we saw more of them as a result.
Our pub trade was a lot more stable in the summertime. We were finding a lot more customers were venturing out from the bigger towns for entertainment and to find us. All sessions were a lot more predictable. Even Monday trade that was virtually non-existent in the early days had become worth our while opening for. Part of the success was probably down to advertising in the local papers 'What's on' pages and some prominent signage placed on the main Canterbury to Hythe road as a guide to our location. I hasten to add I did receive a severe reprimand from the highways department some months later for the 'illegal' posting of the signs. However, I took the slap on the wrist as I felt the signs had served the purpose in the 3 months they were in place before being removed.
Our real ale effort was also proving to be quite successful as well. The local branch of CAMRA had heard of our new offerings and had made several visits to check us out. They were most impressed in what they found and gave recommendations to their members to visit us and try our offerings.

I had taken the opportunity to switch the Ruddles and Burton ales to Wadworths and King and Barnes beers. The pedigree of these new ales had an immediate effect and increased sales accordingly. Phillip was visiting us fortnightly to keep us aware of what was on offer and to advise who was serving what in the area.

In accounting terms, having seen a complete quarter of trading, we had the first opportunity to review the financial performance of the business. I had fully expected and been advised to expect a substantial loss, which is the norm with new fledgling businesses. One would expect a gradual reduction in losses to revert to profit, one would hope, by the end of the first year of trading. Being a strict 'cash only' trade, reconciling one's financial position was comparatively quick and simple. With the aid of dual entry bookkeeping, a daily cash book and till roll receipts to confirm the takings I was over the moon to discover that we had in fact been turning a respectable profit on a sales turnover that was nearing double what our predecessors had achieved. It was a gratifying reward for the efforts we had all put in.

On the downside, we had been in residence long enough to find those areas of the operation and our building that were in need of attention or repair. The chestnut column was one area that had been remedied by Syd. He installed his scrolled screen divider at the same time. It was a work of art and was really well worth doing.

Likewise, the mains changeover wiring had been completed and the new standby generator was in place and ready to go at a moments notice. Till now the weather conditions had been quite favourable and we hadn't experienced any power failures. I got in the habit of running the generator for a few minutes at weekly intervals to ensure its state of readiness. I had also arranged for the electrical inspection to be completed by one of my old specialist electrical subcontractors. Surprisingly, the results of the electrical tests were quite favourable. I was dreading the prospect of a major rewire but was suitably relieved to discover that the existing wiring was safe and should remain so for the next five years. I believe I was lucky with Tom's assistance on that earlier afternoon, and my previous solo efforts, we had rectified those circuits that were dangerous. The other surprise, there were no adverse comments or findings in respect of the continuity and leakage tests carried out on the mains dis-connected system. To this day I am still baffled at what happened when we installed the new bar down lighters!

Other downside issues were discovered, that had to be planned for in advance. The issues needed to be carried out without too much business disruption and to have earned the funds in advance to pay for them.

Firstly, the restaurant extension tiled roof areas were showing signs of leaking. No underfelt had been installed on the shallow pitched roof area and driving rain from a certain direction would leak into the restaurant. It was urgent work with a high priority. I would prefer to have completed the task before the onset of winter.

Secondly, our catering kitchen had recently been inspected by our friendly environmental health officer. We were given a clean bill of health for the time being, but the kitchen fittings were predominantly domestic kitchen units and not really suitable for a modern catering operation. The worktops in particular were the biggest concern; worn and totally unsuitable, requiring urgent attention. The existing floor covering had seen better days and replacement was recommended. The kitchen extraction system was archaic and very inefficient and an upgraded system should be considered. We were however complimented on our selection of cooking range, stand alone appliances and the food storage we had installed. We had purchased the new fryers, bain-marie and main fridge retarder within days of moving in.

Thirdly the main bar area was a bit drab and smoke stained. Redecoration would soon be needed. The carpet was threadbare in places and in a very poor state requiring replacement. The bars were living in the past with 1970's vinyl padding frontage and hideous, character-less Formica tops; all the bars needed updating.

Finally, the overall drainage system was not as efficient as one would hope. Even though the toilet appliances were all modern, quality fittings on occasions they would backup. We experienced similar problems upstairs as well in the shower room and domestic toilet. The septic tank was in sound order but one chamber was slow to empty. The problem would be more evident when we were busy but seemed to disappear when the level of trade was low. Times of high demand were obviously difficult for the system to cope with.

Sue and I agreed we should move on with the restaurant re-roofing operation as quickly as possible. It was hoped that the tiles would be re-used and new felt and tile battens fitted to keep the cost down and maintain the character of the building.

Not that I had the time to carry out the actual work, I felt I could at least supervise and obtain all the necessary materials and equipment to complete the project and in so doing, keep the cost to a minimum. I was sure that from my previous contacts and those made in the pub I would be able to muster the necessary manpower and expertise without having to resort to an expensive roofing contractor. Rod and Smurve immediately sprung to mind. A bit of extra cash may well attract them. Initially they were both interested, but unfortunately, their existing commitments meant I would have to wait for at least another couple of months. Smurve did however suggest a guy from Wye might be able to help. Mark Chimery duly came up to the pub to have a look at the job. He was interested in doing the job but was honest enough to say that Kent peg tiled roofing was his least 'experienced roofing' option. I took it that he hadn't done any such roofing. However he was cheap and available immediately and could also bring Andy his friend to help. Payment terms were strictly cash for both of them. They were both probably signed on I thought, but needs must. It was an unforeseen expense and would not be overly cheap at best. I arranged for tile batten, underfelt, pegs, nails, lead flashing, sand and cement to be delivered. Martin kindly offered to use his staff discount for me to keep the cost down further. Bob loaned me some scaffold tubes, fittings and boards he had stored in the barn opposite and we were ready for the off.

Mark and Andy turned up for work at 8.00am. Initially the three of us constructed a temporary scaffold access platform at eaves level around the three sides of the single storey restaurant extension. I had to leave them to continue on their own shortly after 10.00am to get the bars ready as usual. Sue in the meantime had made bacon sandwiches and tea to keep us all going! The temporary staging was completed by the boys' lunchtime and they came in to the bar for a break. The only time in owning The Dew Drop Inn I allowed a slate to be run up was for those two. Knowing repayment of my money would be safe they indulged in beer and sausage and chips for sustenance.

An hour later and with Sue covering the bar, I went back out with them to start the afternoon work session. The scaffold staging was ideal for amateurs. Boarding was all in the right place and protection provided to the windows below. Even a handrail was fitted preventing anyone walking off the edge. I complimented the two of them and explained how I wanted the stripping work to be undertaken. It was a dirty business to say the least.

Once the tiles were lifted, they had to be cleaned and stacked safely on the platform. The roof area would be open to the elements once the tiles were removed. The secret was to embark on a small area at a time, always keeping an eye on the weather. The battens could than be removed and would be burnt. The rafters could be inspected for any repairs needed and then the new underfelt put in place.

The boys seemed to understand what was expected and started at the front of the building. I once again left them to it and went back behind the bar. I finally went out to see the progress after the last customers left the pub. The twosome was doing really well. The front had been totally stripped of tiles and battens as instructed and they were making inroads into a third of the long flank elevation. The weather was kind with no obvious signs of rain whatsoever. I noticed that the roof void was totally un-insulated so popped back inside to ask Sue to pop into a local DIY store to get some rolls of insulation quilt. I changed into my work clothes and went back to assist. Sue left to pick up the insulation and other essentials.

By the time I had to leave the others to open up, half the roof had been stripped and the void had been insulated with the rolls of insulation Sue had purchased earlier. The underfelt had been unrolled across the rafters of the open roof and temporarily tacked in place allowing for good overlaps at the joins. Some temporary battens were fixed in to keep everything in place. The roof was weathertight albeit under a temporary covering and not the tiles. Time was getting on and the two called it a day. They were both filthy and decided to head off for home.

The following day came and Mark and Andy had made further good progress. By the time I had concluded the bar preparations and ventured outside they had virtually completed the stripping operation. I instructed Mark on the finer points of setting out the new tile battens and left them to it. The remaining roof void was insulated and the new underfelt closed in the gaping hole. This was fortuitous as the cloud had been progressively building throughout the morning. Rain was certainly on the way. The boys took their normal lunch break and as on the previous day ran up their 'repast' on their slate. The re-battening exercise was well in hand and was just about as boring as it gets to complete. Mark had intended finishing the battening operation by the time they were due to knock off. Andy was not coming in the following day so they elected to work on till about seven o'clock. The extra hours helped.

When they finished the bulk of the battening operation had been completed. The little bits that were left were a bit fiddly and were more of a single-handed operation. We were at least completely weathertight under the underfelt. The two called it a day and came in to the bar. I stood them their first pints on the house and settled them up for their first couple of day's efforts. They seemed quite happy with their dues and were in no rush to leave. The bar was quiet and I was happy with the company. It wasn't long till Rod and Smurve turned up. They too had just worked extra hours to meet their target. They were pleased to see Mark and Andy and joined them for a beer. All four were not a pretty sight. They were all dirty and smelt like sweaty jockstraps. They were however having a good time and were spending well to satisfy their thirst needs. By 8.00pm three of them left leaving Smurve alone with me in the bar. He was interested at progress, and as it was still light we went outside and onto the scaffold. Two days in and stripped felted and battened – not bad going as we both agreed. We left the scaffold just as it started to rain. Smurve in the meantime went to his car and got a change of clothes came back in and asked if he could have a wash and brush up. I offered him a shower which he duly accepted.

It was whilst Smurve was in the shower that I noticed water was leaking into the restaurant, above our dresser and alongside the Cona coffee machine. Another little problem had been discovered. I made a mental note to add this latest fault to the 'to do' list. Smurve re-appeared in the bar about twenty minutes later just as our mid-week clientele were pulling on to the car park. There was a full hired mini-bus laden with twelve customers. CAMRA had come up trumps again! Eleven thirsty ale connoisseurs were champing at the bit. I decided a little diplomacy was in order and offered the unfortunate driver free soft drinks on the house for the night. Systematically, our four real ales were put to the test with half pints of each purchased for tasting and analysis. They were all voted top notch, after which it was a free for all for personal choice. Harvey's just took the edge over the other three on the night. It was going to be a difficult decision which beers to change next time around. All twelve guests from our CAMRA cell also ordered food which highlighted how useful and valuable to trade these sorts of visits could be.

Other customers came and went throughout the session, some local some from outside the area. It was most gratifying to bid farewell to our CAMRA visitors just after 11.00pm that night.

They left apparently very happy with the service and beers we had on offer vowing to pass on their recommendation to other cells in the area. In the following months we received no less than four other visits along the same lines we had just seen from different cells in East Kent. Our reputation was spreading and we received the accolade of being one of only seven pubs in Kent to be recommended and added to the CAMRA Great British Beer Guide.

Mark turned up for work the following morning a little later than normal. After leaving the pub they both decided to call in to the Bull on their return to Wye and then the Kings Head in the centre of the village. Mark was nursing a mother of a hangover! Just what he needed with a day of hammering ahead! Understandably, progress slowed on the roof. The infilling and hipped ends took extra time to complete. Lead soakers and cover flashings had to be cut in advance of the re-tiling work. Fiddly and monotonous work, as it was, Mark persevered and finished that section that night. The following day would be re- tiling and the end drawing nearer, tile by tile.

Andy returned the following day with Mark. I took time to instruct the next stage of the work. The bonnet tiles were fitted by Mark whilst Andy fitted the undecloaks along the eaves. The tiling followed hung on new hardwood pegs with every fifth course nailed to the battens. The tiles were positioned to allow broken lap joints which created the impenetrable weather proof layer. The long flank was the easiest to complete first. The returns at either end were a lot more intricate and time consuming. In the event that Andy didn't turn in again I thought it prudent to do the long flank first. Mark agreed with me, almost knowing in advance he would be finishing up single-handed. The side flank was completed that day, just requiring the lead cover flashing to be fitted to the abutment with the wall. The two left at normal time and as expected Andy asked for his money. I paid them up to date again and stood them a round of drinks before opening up. Andy as expected made it clear he wouldn't be in the following day. Mark responded by saying he could finish on his own and Andy would not be required any longer. It was mutually agreed and we parted that evening, Andy not to return, for work anyway. He did however frequent the pub with Mark throughout our ownership of the pub.

Mark finished the re-tiling the following day and spent the Saturday fitting the cover flashing and pointing in cement mortar as required. He finally struck the scaffold and returned the components to the barn opposite. The job was finally finished. A heavy rainstorm tested the new roof out the following day. Inside it was as dry as a bone. It was a relief and a good job done at a very reasonable price.

Mark became a regular Sunday night regular with his father-in law Gordon. Like Clive, they too enjoyed a game of darts in the relative tranquillity and calm of our country pub. Sunday nights were almost becoming regular darts night. It was all good for business!

That Friday night was beneficial in more ways than one for the business. We were busy with a good showing of regulars and diners that kept us busy all night long in all areas of the business. Another young couple arrived at the bar asking to see the landlord. They were total strangers to all of us in the bar. Martin gained my attention and made me aware of the new visitor' request. I excused myself from chatting with Bob, Tom and Sal and approached the couple asking if I could be of assistance. It was quite busy in the bar so I suggested we could go into the restaurant where it was somewhat easier to talk and be heard.

Steve and Deidre introduced themselves as an engaged couple living locally on the outskirts of Ashford. They were saving hard to get married. Steve worked in the local crematorium and Deidre was a cook in the school kitchen at Kennington. They were enquiring about any part-time work opportunities following a visit to the pub by Steve's parents with friends during one of the manic sessions over the previous bank holiday. Deidre's expertise was of immediate interest too me with regard to our intention to offer Sunday Roast lunches. I offered them a drink and went to the bar to get them, poking my head into the kitchen to get Sue to come and join us. Molly could hold the fort temporarily. I returned with the drinks and Sue followed. I introduced her to the couple and asked Deidre to give us a little resume of her experience. She had qualified as a cook through college and took the job for onsite preparation of school lunches for the children. The type and style of food was plain, simple and straightforward. More importantly, one day a week a traditional roast meal was on offer! My guardian angel had answered my wish list! Sue was just as eager about the revelation as I was. I pressed Deidre a little more regarding her roast meal preparation and expertise. It appeared meat was supplied pre-jointed by a major

processor in Ashford. The quality was a bit suspect as the supply price was contracted with the Kent County Council.
The bulk of vegetables were supplied under contract from the same frozen food supplier we were already using. I noted they were lower quality than those that we were using. Deidre worked in a team shift comprising of four cooks under the watchful eye of a supervisor. They were all expected to be multi-disciplined and take a turn at preparation of meat, fish, vegetables and desserts. 'Perfect for us' went through my mind. I then explained our position that primarily we wanted to introduce a Roast Sunday lunch option. A single meat option initially, that could rise to other options if the demand was there. Frozen vegetables initially but moving to fresh in the longer term. It was so far, so good. She was interested. Sue suggested having a look at the kitchen operation. Sue took Deidre to the kitchen and introduced Deidre to Molly and Sara. She appeared impressed at the size and equipment in the kitchen. In the meantime I sounded Steve out. He hadn't had any bar experience in the past but was willing to learn. It was a difficult call. Martin had fitted in well and with my assistance we could cover most eventualities. Smurve was also in reserve most of the time as well. I didn't feel any extra bar support was required so had to let him down. He fully understood my position. Deidre returned from the kitchen by herself. She seemed very eager to give things a go. Sue had to stay in the kitchen as things had got too busy for Molly alone. I explained that a position would be available for Deidre on Sunday morning session to start as soon as practicably possible. It would be subject to a trial period of six weeks. An hourly rate was suggested which was deemed to be very fair. Steve would be kept on a reserve list should another bar staff opportunity arise. They were both delighted and agreed the terms immediately that I offered. I suggested the following Sunday could be a trial run. Deidre was happy to do this without charge to get the feel of the place.
The designated trial day arrived. Sue had picked up a large corner cut topside of beef joint from cash and carry the day before. Deidre was dropped of by Steve to start work. In the kitchen she was obviously well trained and was methodical and meticulous in her food preparation. Deidre had started well before the others turned up for work to allow proper cooking time. The whole pub smelt of the delightful roasting beef aromas. The lovely cooking aromas were complemented by the addition of the customary freshly made coffee

and first batch of baking rolls. Everyone was duly busy with their designated tasks. The telling time came shortly before opening up. Sue and I were in the kitchen. The massive beef joint was done and waiting to be carved. Deidre was more used to using a slicing machine and was a little concerned at carving by hand. Portion control is so important as well as the presentation aspects. Sue volunteered me to do the honours. I initially halved the joint It was cooked to perfection; slightly pink with very little fat. I set about carving the first half. Three plates were set up for the 'dummy run'. Deidre systematically loaded the plates with two slices of beef, a Yorkshire pudding, roast potatoes, peas, carrots and cabbage. Thick gravy topped the lot with a sachet of horseradish on the side. The plated meals were a delight to see.

'That's worth £3.95 of anyone's money!' I exclaimed.

We all agreed and set about tasting one of the plates.

The roast meal was beautiful. Portion sizes were perfect and the meat out of this world. I offered my congratulations to Deidre. She had excelled herself. The successful trial meant not only Sunday Roast lunches but an extended sandwich range and ploughman's could be offered with the 'left over' home cooked meat.

With Deidre's success I decided to get the Roast on the special board as soon as possible. I made Deidre's day by saying she would be paid for the day and a full lunchtime shift was on offer. She agreed and our first lunches were ready to roll.

We had anticipated that the big joint of meat would probably be sufficient for thirty lunches so sufficient vegetables were prepared to cover that number. With it being Sunday additional roast potatoes for the bar had been prepared by Sue and Molly anyway.

Sara had posted the new option on the menu and was ready to open. Martin had finished the bar preparation and so we opened up.

That session was quite memorable. The usual locals and regulars were in as normal. We had a very surprising take up of the Sunday Roast lunches. We were sold out by 1.15pm which was amazing. We looked forward to bigger and better things to come!

Deidre was certainly going to be a major asset for the business.

CHAPTER 9 – Holding it together

The weeks that followed brought about further changes at The Dew Drop Inn. Some for the better, some for the worse! Undoubtedly, one of the highlights had been the introduction of the Sunday Roast lunch which was getting more and more popular by the day. By week three we had found an excellent new supplier of meat and fish products. They were a wholesaler based only a short distance away who dealt directly with both the Smithfield and Billingsgate markets in town. Glen the proprietor had built himself a reputation of supplying quality products in bulk to many of the top hotels and restaurants in the area. Larger joints were never a problem neither what was required. We had switched our specification to exclusive Aberdeen Angus beef on Glen's recommendation. What sound advice that was. Similarly, it increased our capability and so alternative roasts were made available. This change of supplier also had additional benefits as well. Glen delivered directly to the door at no extra cost, the prices were generally considerably lower as any middle man was taken out of the equation and the range of meat, fish, poultry and game on offer was second to none. Latterly, this association formed with Glen was retained as a major strength to the business when 'Bonaparte's' restaurant was floated at the pub some time later.

One of the more negative changes came about unexpectedly. Sara had finished at school having completed her 'A' levels and was looking to go on to university. This didn't fit in with Martin's long term courting plans and led to growing friction between them. Apparently it all came to a head at a Live Music gig they were attending at the Five Bells. Martin apparently tried in vain to tell Sara how she should plan her future out and that didn't include university. Sara was a sensible girl and took the view she hadn't stayed on at school to do 'A' levels and waste the opportunity of going to university. This was too much for Martin and the un-ceremonial parting of the ways duly followed. We later learnt that Jack and Christina were relieved. They didn't seem to see eye to eye with Martin. Martin rang us to explain his break up with Sara and went on to say that working in her presence was completely out of the question. Inadvertently, he put me on the spot by pre-empting a 'him or her' situation. Sara was the more useful employee and would clearly be harder to replace. There was little choice to be considered. I therefore regrettably had to 'accept' Martin's resignation forthwith. Phillip turned up for his normal fortnightly visit. He was clearly excited to tell me about a new development at West Country Products. They had recently undertaken the sole distribution of a very old established brewery in Ringwood in Hampshire. Phillip advised it was one of the smallest brewery operations in the country with a throughput of only 200 barrels, equating to 800 casks a week. In brewing terms this is marginally above micro brewing status. The attraction was that the brewing techniques adopted in Ringwood were as traditional as could be. The resulting beer was a strong, heavily hopped ale and quite dark in colour. Phillip had bought a 2 pint polypin sample for me to try. Old Thumper was the beer's name. I poured a glass to try. It was one of, if not the best beer I believe I had ever tasted. It was gorgeous. Phillip was more than interested to see my reaction and to advise me that if accepted, The Dew Drop Inn would be the first outlet in the South East to stock this beer. Ringwood brewery had outlets for their beer within only a 15 mile radius of the brewery. The brewery was clearly hoping to make a name for themselves by increasing production and distributing further afield.

I was sold on the prospect but was concerned about which beer was going to be substituted. Philip pre-empted the decision by popping out to the van and coming back with another handpump and spear assembly. As I had previously intimated I was prepared to do away with one of the keg bitters – now was the time to do just that. It was down to a straight choice, Webster's or Whitbread Best would have to go. I checked on the reserve stock and found that I had no replacement keg of Webster's and the online keg only had about ten pints left. Webster's was duly knocked on the head. Poor old Phoenix, they had just lost their surviving bitter beer casualty! Philip offered the same terms as usual and made arrangements for 2+1 free Old Thumper casks for delivery on the next consignment. He quickly checked from his records how our sales were doing, compared to other pubs in the area that he supplied. He concluded for his real ale sales we were the top performer in East Kent. There were a couple of other outlets that were bigger and had a lot higher throughput in West Kent. Overall I was more than satisfied to be third in the table, but more importantly number one in East Kent.

Phillip completed the paperwork, shook hands, made his farewell and left.

Bobby delivered the Old Thumper ale with the rest of our order as normal by Friday lunchtime.

She knew of Roscoe's 'strange' behaviour when moving full barrels of beer and always came into the bar to allow the dog to be tied up before venturing through the rear gate. This occasion was no different to any previous. Bobby was very efficient at her job and off loaded the eight cask order. The five replacement casks were put into the beer store and the three Old Thumper casks remaining were left by the back door. The empty casks were collected and loaded onto the dray. Bobby then went and untied Roscoe and engaged in a 'rough and tumble' game with the dog. That was Roscoe's just reward for keeping an eye on the beer!

Bobby finally popped in with the paperwork and for her customary pint. I had just completed the pipe cleaning routine minutes earlier. She had a King and Barnes on this occasion. It was a strong Sussex beer from Heathfield that had affectionately come to be known locally to us as 'Rocket Fuel'. She thoroughly enjoyed the beer and left shortly afterwards.

I went outside to bring two of the new casks into the cellar to cool and settle down. Whilst bringing in the casks I noticed two had green disc stickers on and the remaining one had a pink sticker. What was odd was the filling labels were all of the same date. Strange I thought to myself to have different coding systems. Not to worry, the first green sticker clad cask was taken in, followed by the pink set on top of the other in the cellar. The pink would be opened and used first. I left the cellar and returned to the bar to conclude the installation of the extra handpump. I piped everything back to the cellar and was soon in a position to spile and pre-condition the new beer. I connected the spear fitting and left nature to take its course. The rest of the lunchtime session was quite busy. We had another Age Concern visit from Ashford again bringing a load of old dears on an outing that culminated at the pub for lunch as had previously happened. It was the same driver as before so I stood his lunch and drinks without charge. It was a small gratitude that would keep him and his party returning I hoped! With the session over Molly left having closed down the kitchen. It was a lovely afternoon so I suggested to Sue to take the girls and Roscoe to the beach at

Dymchurch. It was a nice break for us all and to see the sea was a treat.

We returned later that afternoon. It was shortly before 6.00pm as Sue prepared tea for the girls and fed Roscoe. I had a sandwich on the run. I had been in the cellar to see if the new beer was ready. It all appeared fine so went into the bar and pulled the first pint of Old Thumper through.

It was crystal clear, had a beautiful creamy head and smelt heavily of hops and malt. Upon tasting I was in heaven. It seemed to be so much better than the sample Phillip had given me some days before. This really was the crème de la crème of all of our ales. I posted the beer price at £1.20 per pint to see the reaction. Being a little known beer I was quite happy to offer a wine glass sample to un-decided punters. Sara turned in for her shift, giving her side of the break up with Martin. It was the first time we had seen her since. She wasn't in the slightest bit sorry it seemed, and most certainly was not going to allow the break up to affect her working at the pub. In fact Sara had offered to work extra shifts in the week and also behind the bar. She had passed her eighteenth birthday the month previously so was legally of age to do so. I still valued her experience in the restaurant although it did give me an idea for a dedicated restaurant bar to dwell on.

Our Friday night session kicked off well. Friday night regulars and locals were all in early. On seeing the new handpump with its distinctive pump clip interest was aroused. Tom was the first to have a sample and remarked how smooth it was. He even did the unthinkable and had a 'pot' full. The local former students were in after a hard day 'bale carting'. It was totally exhausting work. Jim drove the combine harvester and Bob followed with the baler. The students had to follow behind with tractor and trailer and pick up and stack the bales of straw. Having filled the trailer, it would be transported to one of various open barns on the farm to be re-stacked in the dry for later use. Jim would sell his surplus straw on to specialist merchants once his barns were fully stocked. Very little was wasted in the Little Holt Farm operation. The students found the harvest work tiring and physically demanding. All too often now they would be found in the bar eating and drinking. They were invariably too tired to bother with cooking for themselves so we were a most welcome alternative. They were also keen to keep up with developments. They had finished earlier than normal that night.

Pints of Old Thumper all round seemed to be their choice. It was obviously sweet nectar to their palate after a days grafting in hot and dusty surroundings. The first pints hardly touched the sides as refills were duly ordered. By their own and my submission, we had not tasted anything like it!

As the pace 'hotted up' in the bar I began to miss Martin. I was mindful of keeping customers waiting too long and popped out to find Sue.

The kitchen was ticking over nicely and I suggested Sue could come and help behind the bar for a change. She duly obliged and followed me out. Having realised the Old Thumper was going so well I popped into the cellar and spiled the second cask. The last thing I wanted was to run out and be caught on the hop!

Mark, Gordon his father-in-law and Andy surprised us with a visit that night as well. They too succumbed to the Old Thumper and delighted in the newcomer. Clearly as Phillip had suggested this was extra special, a real winner. He wasn't normally wrong.

The visiting customers from Ashford, Canterbury and Folkestone kept on coming. Both the restaurant and bar operations were moving along very nicely that evening. Steve and Deidre called up with respective parents to have a bar meal. Tom, Steve's father was a bit of a real ale man himself. He was like a child in a 'sweetie shop' with the selection on offer. I gave him a sampler of the new beer. Tom didn't need further convincing. He had one of many pints before the evening closed.

One of the bonuses I discovered with drinking Old Thumper, one rarely suffered hangover symptoms. This was a little surprising as strong bitters can be notoriously 'heady' after a heavy session. I believe there were quite a few drinkers who could confirm that special property that night. By the time we closed that night the pink labelled cask of Old Thumper had only 5-10 pints left. It was just as well the second cask had been spiled. If the beer's popularity was maintained it would be needed early in the lunchtime session the following day.

I was up and about that Saturday morning. There was a lot to get through. Mowing was the first on the agenda. Both our girls were early risers and came out to help. Kate would keep Roscoe amused, whilst Amanda was keen to learn how to use the mower. They took it in turn to learn the rudimentary operation of the little tractor by sitting on my lap, steering and gaining machine awareness. Both girls quickly gained the basics.

They also helped by moving the tables as I passed with the mower and then replaced them in their previous position. We had just finished the grass cutting in the immediate pub areas when Sue appeared vigorously beckoning me inside. I stopped what I was doing and ran inside. A somewhat agitated Phillip was on the telephone. He got straight to the point asking 'Have you got a cask of Old Thumper with a pink sticker on it?' I replied that I had noticed the difference in yesterday's delivery. 'Great, found it!' he seemed relieved. 'I'll be right down in an hour or so to get it!' and rang off. Phillip didn't give me the opportunity to explain that we had used the lions share the night before. I thought about ringing him back to explain but thought better of it. It was obviously important to him and he was probably already on his way. How was I going to explain we had hammered the 'prized' beer cask he was so urgently trying to track down!

I decided it would be easier to keep quiet and went out to the beer store and removed the green sticker and replaced it with the pink one I had removed from the cask in the cellar on the way through. 'What could be so important about a coloured sticker?' I mused and went back to the mowing.

I had finished mowing the village green and gone back inside to complete the normal bar preparation and cleaning procedures when Phillip arrived at the pub. He came in and found me and appeared to be in a far calmer frame of mind.

'Hiya mate! Good to see you!' We shook hands. 'What's the big deal Phillip? You working Saturday...... must be serious!' I queried him. Sara and Molly arrived for the oncoming session.

'Coffee or something stronger?' I offered Phillip 'Coffee would be nice' he replied. Sara had heard and as usual went to put the coffee machine on.

'You've got the pink stickered barrel Pat haven't you?' Phillip confirmed.

'Relax; it's in the beer store. I checked earlier' I replied.

'Thank God. My job would be on the line!' Phillip responded.

'It's the Great British Beer Festival in Leeds, starting next Saturday. Ringwood Brewery is entering Old Thumper. They believe they stand a good chance of winning some sort of award. They sent us a specially prepared cask to go to Leeds. Somehow some idiot in the warehouse sent the bloody thing out on a normal delivery. Thank god you got it!'

Sara brought the coffees in and placed them on the bar.

I just stayed silent and listened intently.

'My director was told what was happening from Ringwood's top man and when my boss went into retrieve the pink labelled cask, guess what, it wasn't there. Shit's been hitting the fan since!'

We drank our coffee then went out to the beer store. Total relief could be seen all over Phillip's face. The illusive beer cask had been found!

I held on to Roscoe whilst Phillip took the cask out to his van. He returned with a replacement cask with a green sticker on. 'I'm so grateful to you mate!' Phillip said. He continued 'I'm in your debt for this. Next delivery and there'll be a little extra!' as he left with the retrieved 'brewery prepared' cask of Old Thumper.

Phillip was true to his word. He had made arrangements to send us two cases of Newquay steam beer, one bitter one lager without charge. They were a completely new concept and style of real ale and lager. The lager was traditionally and not chemically produced. They were totally new to me and seemed quite innovative. It would be interesting to see if there was any interest from the customers.

Some weeks later I was reading the Publican magazine and one of the special features attracted my attention. It was a complete report on the recently staged Great British Beer Festival in Leeds. It was clearly a great success and all the category winners were listed. My eye followed to Best in Class of strong traditional ale. The winner was no less than Old Thumper. I had a little smirk to myself.

Supreme Champion category winner – Old Thumper! I just burst out laughing. This truly confirmed to me the quality of the Old Thumper beer. To be a supreme champion with a bog-standard cask was the epitome of a quality product in its own right!

In recognition of the success in Leeds I added a mock rosette to the pump clip. I believe in the short term that sales of Old Thumper increased as a result!

Our summer season continued un-abated. Another bank holiday was looming at the end of August. We were in the clutches of the main holiday season and our trade levels remained consistently high, regardless whether it was lunchtime or evening sessions. Tom's previous theory had been tested and proved on several occasions throughout the summer – Hot and sunny weekend weather at lunchtime, everyone heads to the coast; we get lower local trade only to be run ragged on the following evening session and really struggle to cope. Holiday visitors to the area were the exception to the rule. It never ceased to amaze me where a lot of our holiday visitors came from. Many of our European cousins were not unsurprising visitors as the close proximity of the Channel port services at Folkestone and Dover allowed ease of access. French, Dutch and German visitors somehow found there way to our pub on a pretty regular basis. Some Nordic visitors had appeared but to a slightly lesser extent.

Americans and Canadians were lured by Canterbury Cathedral. On one occasion we had a visitor from Newfoundland. He could not believe his eyes to see we had one of the dogs that originated from there. It was a great talking point. They came back on another visit to bid us farewell prior to their return back home.

Chinese, Japanese, Singaporean and Arabic visitors had all taken their turn to visit at some time over the summer.

The long summer school holiday also meant that visiting children had suddenly become an added factor and extending the menu to accommodate the little darlings was essential. Accepting the family unit was part and parcel of survival and facilities would have to be provided for the change.

One of the most unpopular additions we made for the older members of the hamlet was the installation of a children's 'Herbie' activity tree. A glass fibre moulded hideous looking tree that provided swings, a slide and play den in one. It basically amused the kids whilst Mum and Dad spent their cash. The close proximity of the school meant the facility was used by children on their way to and from school. Not that we were open at the time it did however entice the children plus parents back during weekend and holiday opening times.

Un-characteristically we hadn't seen sight or sound of Smurve or Rod for a while which seemed a little strange. None of the locals or regulars seemed to be any the wiser either. Sue was on a shopping trip in Folkestone and ran into Rod's wife who informed her both men had fallen foul of being unexpectedly 'laid off'. Apparently there was some sort of legal dispute between the developers of the new shopping parade and the building contractors responsible for its construction. It had been rumoured the developers had gone into receivership and all the works had stopped immediately and 'lay offs' were widespread. It explained why the two men had not been seen of late.

It was in the lead up to the weekend after the Bank Holiday that Smurve made a fleeting visit. It was Thursday lunchtime and he had walked up to the pub from his home. Times were obviously difficult and 'Shanks' Pony' was the cheapest option to get from A to B. Smurve had been trying to find work with little success.

He was a little bit down on entering the bar. I stood him his first pint of Fosters and a bacon sandwich on the house. He confided in me, explaining that the 'lay off' was bad enough but it seems the previous months wages owed to him had been withheld and not paid. Things were looking a bit bleak. Rod was apparently in exactly the same position. Smurve was very proud and would never consider signing on. Whilst we were talking I was mulling over my 'to do list'. I felt that some of those works could be handled by Smurve, and with Martin now gone there was another opportunity there as well. I quickly ran it past Sue who agreed in principle that this could be a bit of a blessing in disguise. I went back to the bar and made Smurve an offer of a joint barman/handyman position. He accepted out of hand and was most relieved in the process. He could start pretty well immediately, particularly as there was still much to do following the Bank Holiday. Schools were still on holiday. He went to leave the pub some time later, a lot happier than how he entered. I got Sue to give him a lift as she was due to head on into town to do a bit of shopping in Ashford. As he left I gave him a sub against his wages as I assumed he would need a bit of cash for petrol. He was deeply grateful for the gesture.

The following morning was pretty busy. Smurve appeared shortly after nine for work. That was ideal as I needed to take him through the pipe cleaning procedure. It was something I had decided I could eventually delegate to him. In the process of showing him what was required I got more of an indication of the mess his laying off had put him in. He had been working extremely long hours in the belief all was well and that non-payment was never an option. He was allegedly owed in the order of £2500 and losing that was obviously a serious blow which he felt understandably bitter about. I had experience in such matters from my previous career and offered advice of how to approach the situation. Company's who indulge in such activities are in my opinion the scourge of the earth and should be pursued with vigour, through the courts if necessary to get some form of equitable satisfaction for the injured parties.

Smurve was completely naive to the ways of the world in this respect and was grateful for the advice and insight.

I explained the Building Contractors were still trading and that a small claims court action should be taken to recoup the debt. Such actions are not expensive and contrary to common belief do not need the services of a solicitor.

Smurve agreed to take my advice and I set the ball rolling on his behalf. For the immediate future I suggested that Smurve should work in a fulltime capacity for us over a five day week with split shifts to cover the morning and evening sessions taking Monday and Tuesday off as his days off. He agreed out of hand which meant Sue and I could tentatively consider making plans to have a regular time off slot without having to close the business. It also meant we would be free to devote a little more time to the family. Molly could handle the midweek catering and Smurve could look after the bar on a regular basis. Sara would always be in reserve if the need arose. All we had to do was hope the punters would keep on coming.

It was quite remarkable how time was flying past and the business development was evolving. For the first time I became aware of customers moving on because parking was becoming an issue. Lost customers invariably meant their trade and money would be going elsewhere; a situation we somehow really needed to address urgently.

Deidre's joining us was proving to be a major boon with the introduction of the Roast Sunday lunches. Our real ale policy seemed to be paying dividends and the continual review and tweaking of the bar food meals we had on offer were just as popular. We were always on the lookout for improvements, or additional services that we could provide to improve our profitability. It was all the more important now as we had committed ourselves to employing longer term staff members.

Time and again as our trade became really busy, parking would become an issue. Smurve noticed the problem as well, and in passing stated the obvious solution. We needed a bigger car park. Both of us looked at the village green and beer garden. The village green was publicly owned and I had no control over it. The beer garden was worth its weight in gold and converting it, or part of it, was impractical. Its loss would reduce the overall customer throughput capability and its awkward shape wouldn't offer that many additional parking spaces either.

Conveniently, I had just managed to sell a little house I owned in Maidstone. The extra money the sale redeemed could help us to find a solution to the parking shortage issue.

I approached Jim with a view to sounding him out if he might consider selling or longer term renting us some land alongside the pub, adjoining the school with an access strip for access from the back lane. The land in question was pretty infertile and in the main overgrown. It struck me, Jim willing, we could provide an extra car parking facility for at least forty cars and an extension to the beer garden, effectively doubling its size. Initially Jim was not overly interested in my proposal. However, Bob heard about the idea and got Jim to re-consider. The parcel of land extended to just under an acre and at the time would have been worth in the order of £2000 as prime agricultural land. As it was and in its current state it was barely worth half that amount.

Jim felt it was not worth his while to part with it for such a derisory amount. Legal fees taken out he would have been lucky to have seen £800. In fairness I would have probably taken the same view. However, the value of the land was obviously higher to the pub for the extended facilities. I offered to purchase the land for £2500 and pay the legal and fencing costs. Jim was surprised at the generous offer and agreed to the sale. The sale only took three weeks to conclude and I wanted to proceed with the car park and garden extension at the first opportunity.

On this occasion I enlisted extra support as before. Rod and Mark were happy to carry out the fencing work which was a load off my mind. I hired a large excavator, dumper and roller through my old contacts and took on the car park works with Smurve. We worked flat out removing topsoil and regrading the area for the car park and access road. The machines were running incessantly. Tom came over and assisted on a couple of occasions as well. Whilst I had the big excavator I decided to investigate the ground around the outfall of the septic tank. It didn't take long to discover the cause of our drainage back up problem. The outfall pipe had been broken that led to the 'herringbone' underground filtration system. Effluent from the septic tank couldn't run away hence at times of high demand the system backed up. We dug a new enormous deep soakaway for effluent disposal in the extended garden area and connected it too the septic tank. Our below drainage problems were solved at a stroke. The rest of the car park was hardcored and compacted to falls and crossfalls and finished with clinker ash that looked like tarmac but was completely free draining. All the works were completed within the 7 day hire period of the machines. I added some extra finishing touches with floodlighting and an access path to the pub. It was the best thing we could have done for the business. By the time I had paid all the material bills, labour and plant bills we had change from £7500 and that included the land as well. It was a major improvement and worth every penny! Never again should we lose business because of the shortage of parking space. The local residents were happy with the addition as well. Access problems and double parking should now be a thing of the past.

We were both grateful for Smurve's extra efforts with the car park and paid an ex-gratia bonus to him. He was really grateful for the extra £150 we paid him. It was the first of many jobs we undertook together. We managed to work around the trading sessions quite well with the minimum of disruption to the business or our customers. On occasions Smurve had become accustomed to 'staying over' at the pub to enable us to complete a job done to schedule. He had his sleeping bag and was perfectly happy to stay in the bar overnight. It also meant that drink driving was not a problem for him!

CHAPTER 10 – Taking a breather

The month of September is a significant time of year. Its arrival heralds some key events in a publican's calendar. The early days signify the return to school after the long summer holidays and a noticeable turndown in trade follows as a result. Families become weekend visitors, rarely seen during the week. The walkers and ramblers seem to don their boots and cagoules to make the most of the early autumnal weather. The hop harvest is normally concluded by the middle of the month with brewers starting their autumn offerings of new season ales. There were further changes planned at The Dew Drop Inn.

With the anticipated drop off in business we all agreed a sprucing up exercise was in order to enhance our presentation to the public. The main bar was dingier than ever with smoke-staining being the major culprit. The bar's retro look was well beyond its sell by date and required something to enhance the charm of the old place.

Smurve and I looked at completing the works as best as possible on the run and came up with various ideas for the makeover, to be presented to the lady of the house for her blessing. As always, cost had to be strictly controlled, which limited our scheme dramatically. The key areas for attention were highlighted. The bars needed a complete makeover with something to create a 'wow' factor. The coloured hideous obscured glass in the windows throughout needed to be changed. The old barstools and seating had seen better days and needed changing or refurbishing. A complete redecoration was required and new carpets were to be laid. Conveniently, having our bar area in two separate halves meant we could alternate the work between areas whilst keeping open for trade. We allocated tasks between ourselves. Smurve would undertake the re-glazing. Sue would decide on a new colour scheme and get an idea of the new carpets. I tasked myself with the bar makeover. We all decided the furniture re-furbishing would be jointly sorted out or by other means. Smurve used his contacts to obtain the new glass. We had decided a clear top pane with a modern, flemished pattern lower pane throughout. The resultant effect was to allow more light in and make the bar lighter. Being a successful glazier by trade, Smurve was in his element and reckoned the whole reglazing operation would only take 3-4 days at the worst and that included the restaurant windows as well. Everything was in good hands and under control with Smurve in charge.

Mark's brother had been to the pub on a couple of occasions with the others for the Sunday night un-official darts competition. Conveniently he ran a flooring business and offered advice on the type of carpet we should consider. There probably isn't a more hostile or hardwearing situation for a carpet existence than an old country pub.

Paul recommended an 80% woollen and 20% nylon mix Wilton carpet on a sound rubber underlay. He also maintained that coir brush matting within the entrance porch areas and immediately around the front of the bar would reduce the overall wear on the carpet significantly. Sue had decided on a classical small crested pattern in a dirty pink colour with black coir matting. They looked a good match. Paul came up with an acceptable quote for the work and was told to proceed and obtain the material for later installation.

In the meantime I removed all of the former red vinyl buttoned bar front, exposing the original substrate, which was old tongue and groove panelling. Its overall condition was fine at the upper level end and I decided to thoroughly sand back and re-stain the bar front and finish with a velvet sheen lacquer. The lower bar was not in the same condition. Chestnut pales were cut and fixed vertically to the exiting boarding, stained and finished as the upper bar. A different, rustic country feel was created in this area. The 'piece de resistance' was a new smooth overlaid polished copper bar top. It looked the business! The downlighter canopy ceiling was lined and papered with hessian wallpaper and the face of the wrought iron glass rack was covered with new natural hops that were illuminated from behind. It was a simple makeover with clean lines that was relatively cheap, didn't take that long to do. and made a difference that was staggering.

We finished by redecorating throughout with buttermilk walls and a mushroom ceiling between the ceiling beams. This lightened and transformed the whole place.

The old exposed beams were given a re-stain. Paul finished up on the Friday by laying the carpets and coir mats. By the time of the evening session the bar was completed and ready to go on show. The punters loved it! Only the seating makeover was incomplete.

Whilst the makeover was in hand I couldn't help but notice our stocks of chocolate bars seemed to be inexplicably reducing.

They weren't massive profit earners for us but I started to get a little concerned that they may well have been being thieved. They sat at the end of the lower bar with the other confectionary we stocked and could have been easily taken by someone when the bar staff were not looking. Smurve had noticed the same stock reduction without actually recalling making any sales. It was strange as it only applied to the milk chocolate, hazel nut and fruit and nut bars. Twix, kit-kat and marathon bars nearest the front of the display were un-affected.

The solution was discovered early one morning when Smurve had stayed over in the bar. Completely unaware of Smurve's presence, our youngest daughter Kate came down from upstairs having readied herself for school. She had gone to the back door and opened it to allow Roscoe in behind the bar. Being quite short, and only 6 at the time, she got the dog to sit in the doorway. Always obedient for Kate, Roscoe did exactly as he was told. Kate moved the barstool to the confectionary display and climbed on to the stool. Turning to Roscoe she asked him
'So what would you like today, Rossie?'
Thinking she had made the right decision she would hold up the selected chocolate bar for the dogs reaction.
'Woof' would be Roscoe's response. She would climb off the stool, replace it and open the bar wrapper. Breaking a piece of chocolate off Kate would offer it to the dog.
'Say please...'
'Woof' the dog would 'answer', still obediently sat down with a paw upraised to be rewarded with the chocolate treat.
This action would be repeated until the chocolate had gone followed by Kate returning the dog to the garden. This performance was completed in total oblivion of Smurve's presence, who found to amusing to say the least.
Later that morning whilst having a coffee, Smurve enlightened Sue and me.
'Solved the missing choccy bars!' he said 'A great big black 'orrible thing came in the bar early this morning.' He mused. We both looked at each other strangely.
'Go on' Sue said.
'Young Kate, bold as brass lets the dog in and gives him his treat. He has to earn it mind you!' Smurve finished.
'Cheeky little mare!' Sue replied.

Deep down we all thought it was funny. It also explained how Kate had bonded so well with Roscoe!

Having completed the bar makeover and refit our level of trade stabilised. The new car park facility was a really useful addition. As we had hoped at peak periods the extra car parking capacity enabled us to continue with the minimum of criticism from other residents in the hamlet. Returning customers were amazed to see the changes that had been completed over the summer. Not a single derogatory comment was heard.

With the onset of autumn, we had to re-light the fires in the bar and restaurant inglenooks. It was an extra expense but was well worth it for the extra cosy atmosphere the fires generated. The bar fireplace had electric lights fitted inside to highlight the beaten copper hood. We changed the clear bulbs for red ones that immediately gave an added sense of warmth without any extra expense. These little touches were proving to be so beneficial.

The only remaining makeover item yet to be finished was finally resolved. The bar stools on inspection, really were beyond their useful lifespan. We ordered new high and standard stools for the bar from a specialist furniture supplier. They were not immediate stock items and were delivered two weeks after the initial unveiling. We also purchased some matching Dralon fabric to re-upholster the seat cushions of the pew style seating that was retained.

Our daily and weekly routine was now really well organised. Monday's had become known as the 'refresh' day. Along with the banking, Sue would make the customary Cash and Carry run for restocking from the weekend. Molly by now was very proficient in the kitchen. The bar and restaurant 'deep clean' through would be part of the normal timetable and normally undertaken by yours truly. Initial deliveries would be made from the frozen food supplier and our new supplier Allied Brewery. Phoenix' service just got worse so a change was inevitable. Allied offered us more than double the discount Phoenix were giving us which was the final straw. We would have been fools to have stayed with Phoenix.

Our homemade soups had also improved from the early days. With the Sunday Lunch option now well established Deidre would ensure that 'leftovers' would never go to waste. Meat offcuts and unused vegetables would all be saved for Molly to use in our range of homemade soups. Cooking stock would be left to cool on the side for later use in one of our large catering saucepans. Monday morning would be the designated time to make the soups in bulk and chill or freeze for later consumption. Monday was also ideal because with the holiday season over, the lunchtime session reverted to being the quietest of the week. There were exceptions to the rule of course. Since having Smurve on our permanent staff, my 'to do' list was becoming shorter as time passed by. Three of the four main items had been attended to. The lesser items were slowly getting done. The leaking shower above the restaurant appeared to be getting worse all the time. It was once an occasional drip that had become a distinct dribble when the shower was in use. Trying to pinpoint the leak was the problem. The shower had been completely built in and tiled. The sealant strips within the cubicle all appeared in good condition. They certainly didn't appear to be leaking. The leak must have been within the tray itself, the trap, or the pipework that drained the shower to the external soil stack underneath. The tray was a one piece, fibreglass moulded unit with no means of access. The only way to trace the fault would necessitate either removing a section of floor, or the ceiling directly beneath in the restaurant. Providing the shower was not used during opening hours it wasn't a serious issue. When we were closed we got in the habit of putting a collecting vessel on the dresser beneath the leak. As Molly worked hours that coincided with the pub being open she was totally unaware of the leaking shower problem.

Unusually, on this particular Monday we were to receive a walking party of about 40 from the Hythe Active Retirement Association (HARA). Like many of their predecessors, rural pubs would be targeted to visit with a view to using their facilities for an organised ramble in the area. Their organiser had been in contact with me the week before to make the necessary arrangements over the phone and seek my agreement to allow the party to use our car parking facilities. I had agreed unreservedly, just asking them to use the new car park to the side of the pub and not the village green. The organiser also asked if we could provide bar meals on a pre-ordered basis on the day. I assured him that there would not be a problem. So as to avoid any embarrassment, I made the point that house rules did not allow food, other than that purchased at the pub to be consumed on the premises. Everything was agreed and menus for personal selection would be made available on the day.

Molly was aware of the ramblers due that day and came in early. Sue had already left for the cash and carry trip. The banking was going to be done later that day. I was engrossed in the cleaning operation when Molly arrived. She went and made coffee for both of us and came out to ask what was to be done.

'We'll have Minestrone soup today. You do remember how to make it?'

Molly nodded to the affirmative and headed back to the kitchen. She stopped and turned back, sensing I was about to say something.

'There's smoked bacon in the bottom of the fridge and yesterdays veg there to use as well. Deidre left the stock on the side. We've got 40 odd in for lunch so make a large batch.' I continued.

'Oke-dokey Pat.' she replied and went into the kitchen.

I took my coffee out to the bar to continue with the opening preparations.

Right on eleven o'clock and with military precision the HARA convoy arrived. There were about sixteen cars in all, and as requested they all followed round to the rear of the pub and into our new car park. Some had been to the pub before and were suitably surprised at seeing the new improved facility.

I went out to greet the walkers and took the menus for them to make their selection. I explained that everything was available and that the homemade soup of the day was Minestrone. That appeared to go down very well. I left the visitors mulling over their selection and returned to my labours in the bar. The organiser had agreed he would return the order and menus when ready.

Allied's dray delivered shortly afterwards dropping off my keg beer and crate order. Their draymen refused to go through the back gate with the barrels for fear of being eaten alive by Roscoe. As was the norm Roscoe was barking through the gate at his best. Empties were quickly loaded and the two draymen came in to collect a signature for the delivery. Unusually, they thanked me for the offer of a drink but declined even a soft one or coffee. To this day I don't recall those guys ever accepting a drink ever.

By the time the brewery delivery formalities were dealt with the party organiser had returned with the all important order selection. I cast my eyes down the listing. No less than thirty-one had selected the Minestrone soup of the day. There were twenty-seven meals in addition of various selections and a note that coffee would also be required but no specific number given.

'Not a problem I confirmed. Ready 1.30pm?' I asked.

'Champion' the organiser replied.

'We'll set your party up in the restaurant alright?'
'That'll be fine.' he acknowledged and then left.
It was now after twelve and the bar should have been open. I had not completed all the cleaning and opened up fully intending to complete the procedures on the run. I had showered earlier that morning in case of this eventuality. I was just concluding polishing the copper top bar when Molly popped in.
'What's occurring?' she asked
'Order's on the side there Molly. They want over 30 soups. You've done plenty?'
'Oh yes, I think so!' she replied unperturbed
'Right I'll get on with this then!' Molly took the list and went back to the kitchen.
I finished up all the cleaning procedures and went behind the bar. Molly had put the coffee on as normal and rolls in the oven. The usual cooking combined aromas were eking into the bar as normal. Everything smelt divine. I pulled through the five real ales and checked them all. As we were quiet and Molly appeared to have everything in the kitchen under control I headed out the back door and tied Roscoe up so I could bring the latest beer delivery through the back gate and into the beer store. Roscoe was not mused. I was messing with his barrels and he couldn't get near me! He just barked his lack of amusement. Ten minutes later he was off the lead and I had got everything in.
I shouted to Molly if everything was alright from the back garden. She gave me the thumbs up so I went back behind the bar. Sue still hadn't returned. I had rather hoped she would be back by now.
Our first customers appeared. They parked on the village green and came in. They had been before but not seen the pub after its latest improvements. I served them their drinks and they ordered a couple of ploughmen's meals in addition. I took the order to the kitchen and gave it to Molly. She was extremely well organised. One of our massive catering saucepans was on the range simmering away. The soup contents looked and smelt fabulous. Bowls and plates were all laid out ready to be loaded. Salad garnishes were all prepared on plates. Molly took it all in her stride. I quickly returned to the bar as more visiting customers turned up.
The new foursome, two couples selected two pints of Old Thumper for the men and two halves for their female companions. I served the beers and noticed Sue had just arrived back home.

'About time too!' I was thinking

'What a lovely beer.' The first man commented.

'It was Supreme Champion at Leeds!' I explained proudly. I wanted to tell my tale but left them all to savour the flavour.

Molly came in with the two ploughmen's and served them to the waiting customers.

Sue appeared behind the bar to find out what was happening. I told her everything was in hand but the main party of walkers would be back at any minute. Molly was completely in control in the kitchen. Sue left and went to unpack the supplies from the car she had just collected.

The leader of the foursome came to the bar and ordered four jumbo cod, chips and peas and asked if their meal could be taken in the restaurant. I explained they were welcome to do so but there was a large party due at any second. I thought it may be better to stay in the bar. He accepted my explanation, paid and went back to the others.

The faster ramblers appeared ahead of the main party. There were initially ten who ordered mainly soft drinks and went through. Molly met them, showed them to their table and got the serving up operation under way. Sue finished unloading and asked what to do. I explained that the remaining thirty members of the HARA party were here and perhaps it would help if she could serve behind the bar initially, then once the majority had gone into the restaurant go an assist Molly.

The walkers had returned and were coming in fast and furious. Sue and I were serving as fast as possible. Everyone appeared to like the surroundings. Those customers who had been before remarked on what an improvement had been made. Once they had been served I tried to encourage the visitors to pass on through to the restaurant. Molly showed the next batch of customers to their tables and went back to the kitchen.

Sue left and went to assist Molly. The four fish meals for the bar were next to come out. Sue served them asking if any additional condiments were required. They were very happy and declined Sue's offer.

The leader man gained my attention and asked for a repeat performance of the previous round. I nodded and started to pull their beers in between the final customers from HARA.

Molly in the meantime was ladling the soup into bowls as Sue placed freshly baked rolls on to the plates Molly had prepared earlier. Soup bowls were collected with the rolls and taken out to the waiting customers. It was all very mechanical and the girls were extremely efficient.

I had served the last of the HARA customers and taken the Old Thumper beers to the foursome who thanked me in return. I asked if everything was to their liking and received their collective compliments. I cleared the couple's plates that had the ploughman's meals earlier and found them just as complimentary. They asked for two coffees which I collected on my return from taking the dishes to the kitchen. I was relieved to note the HARA party were all seated and appeared to be enjoying themselves. Those people who had ordered soup had been served and the girls were now following up with the main meals. On the surface of it, everyone was very happy with the service and our offerings.

Two other cars pulled onto the front car park. One I recognised as Smurve'. He came into the bar. He was aware of the rambler's party but didn't appreciate it was so big.

'You should've rung me mate!' he said having seen how many were 'in'.

'No problem. It's your day off. That's important.' I replied as I pulled his pint of amber nectar. Invariably Smurve came to the pub on his days off anyway.

'Here I got this today!' Smurve said passing me a letter he had received.

It was a letter from the court stating that his former employer had responded to the small claim writ served against them. They had accepted the debt, including the court cost and paid the dues into court. Attached to the back of the letter was the court cheque made out in favour of Smurve.

I was delighted. In my opinion there is nothing worse in life than 'bully boy' tactics.

Smurve was over the moon and bought me a drink to celebrate.

Four more people came in from the second car. They wondered if we were still serving food. I advised we were and offered them the menus and referred them to the Specials Board as well.

They ordered their drinks whilst making their food selection. An All day breakfast, ham eggs and chips, jumbo cod and chips and a fisherman's platter were chosen. The same request was made to eat in the restaurant to which I offered the same reply. It certainly was quite noisy in there. The party decided to stay in the bar and seated themselves accordingly. I took the order to the kitchen and noticed that all the HARA meals had been served. Molly took the order and got it underway.

As I left the kitchen Sue caught my attention and wanted a private word. She had been a little confused. She had been serving coffee to the earlier diners of the HARA party and noticed the large saucepan collecting the leaking shower water had been moved. It wasn't by the coffee machine. Where had I put it? She also noted that the stock that Deidre had left in the larder in a saucepan was still there. Molly apparently hadn't used it in the Minestrone soup she had made earlier. The vegetables from the fridge and bacon had all been used up. I wasn't sure what she was driving at and had to return to the bar as the bell had been rung to attract service.

On returning to the bar it was in fact the organiser of the HARA party. He explained that they were shortly to be leaving. Each customer would be settling their dues as they left. I thanked him for the business. He in turn thanked me and made a point of saying other HARA members would be told of our existence and they would return. He settled his dues and left. From there on in there was a steady flow of the remaining customers leaving.

Sue returned to the bar with the party of four's meals. They were most impressed with what was prepared for them and tucked in.

An elderly couple came from the restaurant to settle their bill for the meal they had earlier. They were two of the customers who had just the Minestrone soup and roll.

'We're really delighted. Delicious homemade soup.' the old gentleman commented.

'Best Minestrone soup I've ever had!' his wife confirmed.

'Is the lady cook who served us available?' they asked.

'One moment Sir' I replied and dodged out to the kitchen.

'Molly, your fan club wants a word. C'mon quickly, they're in the bar!' I joked with her

'She's just coming.' I told the old couple as I returned to the bar. I took their money and gave them their change as Molly appeared.

'Thank you so much for the best Minestrone soup we've ever had!' they said to Molly and gave her a pound tip.

Molly was touched, thanked them and went back to the kitchen. The old couple left shortly afterwards.

Smurve heard the earlier compliment, smiled to himself and asked for another pint. I duly obliged and had a chuckle. 'Who'd have thought that?' I said putting his recharged glass on the bar.
The bar and restaurant started to empty quite quickly and trade started to slow dramatically. The last of the HARA party left shortly after 2.30pm. They all seemed just as happy.
The late arriving foursome had coffees all round and were away shortly before 3.00pm. We shut up shop, turned the lights off and relaxed in the bar after our efforts.
I was still a little perplexed at Sue's confusion earlier, more importantly how the previous day's stock hadn't been used. I asked Molly outright.
'Why didn't you use the stock from Sunday in the soup Molly?' I asked.
'I did' she replied.
'Were there two pans then?' I went on.
'No, there was just the one pan.' Molly seemed a little quizzical.
Sue interjected by saying the stock was in the larder.
Molly said she didn't know about that.
'I took the bacon and vegetables from the fridge, like you said Pat and, as you said made a large pan, enough for 40 odd with the stock that was in the big pan on the dresser in the restaurant.'
Sue and I couldn't believe our ears.
Molly had clearly misunderstood the earlier instructions I had given and thought the previous day's vegetable stock was in the pan on the dresser in the restaurant, which in reality was the collected overflow liquid. She had only gone and made the Minestrone soup from our second hand shower water!
Molly, Sue and I were gob smacked at the reality of the situation.
What should we do?
In reality there was little we could do.
Smurve concluded the discussion by offering his opinion
'The soup must have been good though. The old boy and girl loved it and gave Molly that tip as well!'
Once over the initial shock we all fell about laughing. Needless to say the leftover soup was disposed of!

CHAPTER 11 – Keeping momentum going

The rural location of our home was beautiful at anytime but in October with the full onset of autumn, Mother Nature's colour transformation was nothing short of spectacular. Gone were the vivid greens of summer, to be replaced with autumnal shades of gold, orange and browns, contrasting starkly with the chalky soils and parallel ploughed field furrows. Early morning mist would settle in the hollows giving an air of mystic and magic to the scene. The sun would glint through heavily dew laden spiders webs spun between branches of bushes and in the hedgerows. It was my favourite time of the year that would be relatively short-lived in preparation for the dreary winter months that followed.

The level of business trade could be a little erratic at this time requiring an element of ingenuity to keep ahead of the competition. In our case the usual busy spells were now well entrenched and established. However, extra interest to attract the new visitor was always in our minds.

Going hand in glove with ploughing match events was the start of the shooting season in the countryside. Pheasant and fowl shoots were generally for the gentry at very expensive locations, well beyond the means of normal country folk. Pigeon and rooks were more common sport for the average country dweller, normally at the invitation of local farmers as a means of pest control. Jim was no exception to the norm. He and Bob would experience problems first hand with crop damage as a result of pigeons and crows attacking the spring and winter wheat crops as they struggled to establish themselves. This had given me the idea for an added service we could offer that could attract more business.

Shortly after we moved to our country pub I applied for a new shotgun licence which was duly awarded to me covering the two shotguns I subsequently purchased. Tom and I had been out on several occasions with Jim and Bob around the farm, to cull the pigeon and rooks that could breed and give rise to an increase in population, exacerbating the crop damage problem. It was quite enjoyable and further helped in my acceptance to becoming a true 'country boy'.

It was following one of these shooting trips that I sounded out Sunday lunchtime customer's interest in my idea of a regular clay pigeon shooting competition. I was surprised to find a high level of interest in my proposal. Most pubs have dart teams, pool teams, skittle teams why not have a clay pigeon shoot? Jim was more than happy for us to shoot out over his land from the elevated garden area. It was a spectacular vantage point looking out over the valley with un-interrupted views and ideal for my proposal. The trap positioning meant all spread of patterns could be launched, testing the most ardent gun! Any missed clays would degrade naturally once they returned to terra firma and be ploughed in.

I visited my local gunsmith in Canterbury and sought out a suitable clay pigeon trap launcher and a stock of different clays. The launcher could throw dual pairs of clays at once or just singles at will. Smurve and I put down a concrete base for the trap to be sited on as a permanent site. Four gun peg positions were marked out and we were ready for our first session.

We advertised the inaugural clay shooting match for the second Saturday morning in October commencing at 11.00am and to be repeated fortnightly thereafter as long as the demand remained. The intention was to have a morning competition until 1.00pm and then adjourn for lunch. The purpose of the exercise was to attract custom to the pub from the competitors, and when word got about, attract more competitors from further afield.

I decided that an entrance fee of £5.00 would be charged covering the cost of the clays and a prize pot for the outright winner. Entrants would use their own guns and cartridges, although I was happy to 'rent' my second gun and cartridges to those entrants wishing to take part, but did not own a gun.

The day duly arrived and I was very happy to note the interest. I left Smurve to look after the bar in my absence and headed out to the garden. It was a brilliant sunny morning, a bit chilly but still air and perfect for clay pigeon shooting.

Virtually all the male locals and regulars turned out for the occasion. Local farm workers and friends also appeared, presumably through hearing about the event via word and mouth. In all, there were twenty-one of us taking part which provided a winners pot of £50. It was fascinating to see the range of hardware that was brought out for the occasion. Single barrels, double barrels, under and over, poacher and pump-action guns were all on show. Modern and old alike – hammer and enclosed actions for all to see. Some guns were on their first and only outing of the year, some well used on a virtual daily basis. Tom brought over his grandfathers old 410 hammer action double barrel gun that was 120 years old. Tom reckoned it was the best gun he had ever shot with.

Colin was there brandishing one of a pair of Purdy guns he owned – truly magnificent firearms with the most elaborate and detailed engraving I have ever seen, and with a price tag of in excess of £10,000.00 each!

We got underway with the initial practice round of the competition. Lots were drawn for gun positions and I operated the trap. Initially, I threw large clays that travelled a lot slower to enable the guns to get their eyes in. Each person had three 'practice' clays before changing over to the next foursome. The competition started after the warm up. We shot in pairs which meant that in the competition rounds, two clays had to be hit in a single pass with a total of five scoring rounds, a total of ten clays thrown per contestant. Each gun had to be given a mix of 5 large and 5 clays. As the launcher I determined what mix of clays was thrown.

Tom, Jim and Rod made the early running. Rod used my poacher under and over gun. It was lighter and arguably easier to track the faster smaller clays. Tom was consistent with his old 410. Jim sported a pump-action reloader. Ironically, Colin with his Purdy, by far the most superior of the hardware, couldn't hit the 'barn door' if it was closed in front of him! Despite all of his excuses, he only managed two 'kills' from the ten clays and they were 'wingers', a lucky pellet making random contact!

In the final reckoning there was a tie between Jim and Rod necessitating a final 'shoot-off'. It was an instant death competition. First person to miss their pair was the loser.

Jim was the ultimate winner on the third pair and was duly awarded the £50 pot.

We all retired to the bar whereby Jim stood the first round on his winnings. Overall the event was a great success. In the days that followed the word spread and the event taking place two weeks later was to be even more successful.

As I had hoped, the Saturday Clay Shoot had been a success in more ways than one. The level of trade proved to be somewhat higher than the norm in both wet and food sales.

Steve and Deidre had become regular users of the pub during the week since Deidre joined our team. She had fitted in well and the Sunday roast lunches had become a firm favourite, particularly as we were now offering a choice of two roasts on a permanent basis. Now that the Sunday Roast had become a normal feature, Deidre was looking for more hours to work.

It had crossed my mind to extend the roast concept to the Saturday evening but somehow both Sue and I felt it didn't seem quite right to do so. Ironically, it was Glen who had the solution to our dilemma. He had recently started supplying to the new tenants at the George Inn on Stone Street, about four miles away. The George Inn had a very chequered history. A lovely old brewery owned pub, but unable to sustain a regular landlord so it seemed. The tenants would change very regularly; every 3-6 months appeared to be the norm. The new incumbents were trying to attract trade by offering massive 56oz 'T-bone' steaks! This wasn't what I had in mind but seeing the earlier success of the likes of the steakhouse chains I thought this might be the way forward. Glen could offer us Aberdeen Angus beef steaks, cut and trimmed to specific size, specification and cryo-vac wrapped for prolonged storage and extra maturing of the meat. This method of storage also enabled us to increase our order size to benefit from lower prices.

Steak sales are far more attractive because they command a higher sales price and margin. Due to their popularity, the public at large generally don't mind paying the extra either. It was however imperative that quality standards were maintained. The higher the quality, the more profit could be made. Aberdeen Angus beef I believe commands the highest hallmark in beef production. This could also enable us to take the restaurant a little further up-market by offering steaks exclusively in the restaurant surrounding and charging the premium price accordingly.

I discussed the option with Deidre, impressing the quality and standards expected. She loved the prospect of the challenge and the opportunity to earn extra cash in the process.

I ordered two dozen of each rump and sirloin steaks from Glen for delivery on the following Thursday and made arrangements for Deidre to work the Saturday night, primarily as our grill chef. Molly would still handle the bar meals. Sara would initially have restaurant clientele for both menus but we would try to encourage the steak options over the bar meal menu to increase the restaurant profitability. Like the steakhouses, chips, peas, mushrooms, onion rings and tomato would be the steak accompaniment and an ice cream dessert was included in the price. £6.50 and £6.95 were the initial prices charged for rump and sirloin options with an ice cream dessert respectively.

Our initial venture on the first Saturday night was quite successful. We managed sales of 20 rumps and 18 sirloins which was most encouraging. Deidre had done well, as had Molly with her 40+ bar meals. The profit return on the steaks was virtually double that of the bar meals. Clearly, encouraging the steakhouse option was the direction we had to take. Extending the steak menu to encompass fillet and 'T-bone' steaks would also be beneficial to us, we thought. Both Sue and I were really encouraged with the initial steak venture and decided to go all out for the extended option. Glen also gave us extra 'food for thought' for the new range of special pre-prepared range of chilled meals he had access too. Beef and chicken curries, beef stroganoff, chilli con carne and beef hotpot were all on offer as high quality products, requiring re-heating, vegetable addition, plating and serving. Extremely competitively priced, this range of products were clearly going to provide additional choice on the daily specials boards as the colder winter days drew near. We had samples provided by Glen for our consideration. The curry's and stroganoff were of particular interest. As we were led to believe, they were high quality, great tasting and really good value for money.

The changes kept on coming at The Dew Drop Inn!

The venue and timing of our second 'clay shoot' contest appeared to have spread far and wide. In the days leading up to it we had countless telephone enquiries from impending entrants from within a 10 mile radius. The size of winner's pot seemed to be the biggest lure. Clearly we couldn't be precise but suggested it would be between £50 and £100 with an entrance fee as before at £5. Clay pigeon competitions, like ploughing matches are part of the regular country scene at this time of year. There is absolutely no doubt that the real characters of the countryside will appear at most, if not all of these events. In their own charismatic and distinctive styles they will blend into the rural backdrop, taking the backseat and keeping a low profile until their moment comes. Then and only then does their prowess and expertise come to the forefront in whatever discipline they could command.

Trevor Keats, TK to those who knew him was one such character. Raised from Romany stock, TK was mature in years. Tom maintained TK was two years his senior. TK emphatically denied Tom's 'slanderous' accusation. He was a rough diamond and a lovable rogue, although he did have a somewhat debatable reputation towards the quality of his work and reliability angle.

Being from a hardened life background he lived in a small caravan that went everywhere he did, pulled behind his old army surplus Landrover, and bedecked with the tools of his trade, he was a tarmac layer by trade. TK was as far as we were aware a long-term bachelor and was always accompanied wherever he went by his two dogs; a small Jack Russell terrier and an Irish lurcher. He also had an unbelievable attraction to the younger female sex. Whatever it was that appealed, TK would normally always be seen out entertaining with a couple of mid-twenties, blonde, gorgeous, classy and beautiful women.

His eccentricity extended to his attire. During the day he would be seen wearing his typical working country clothes. Corduroy trousers, collarless shirt under a black sleeveless waistcoat open almost to the waist to expose his unbelievably, grey hairy chest under an enormous wide brimmed floppy felt hat. The hat was probably a relic from the early seventies, probably worn by some pot smoking and spaced out 'hippychick'.

Come sundown, TK would change and be seen out regularly dressed in a collarless shirt, open to expose his hairy chest, a maroon satin cummerbund; Levi flared jeans and either a white or black tuxedo dinner jacket of which he owned both. The hat would be replaced by a red and white headdress, allegedly given to him by a grateful sheikh customer but looked more distinctly like an old tasselled, chequered curtain. To finish off TK would normally have a blonde beauty on either arm, always dressed impeccably.

He was a true character when he wanted to be. He spoke with a typical Kentish country accent and unlike most similar types; TK would rarely swear or blaspheme. He could drink like a fish but would rarely get out of hand. There was never any sign of a vicious streak in the man, drunk or sober! His companions loved his company and responded to all his dramas and play acting. TK was an amusing showman and performer and could recount a host of country life experiences. Whether they were true or not was another matter! He would be the best of customers, spending like there was no tomorrow, but only after being given permission to park up his caravan and Landrover for the night where he would eventually retire to. To this day I'm not entirely sure what happened to his companions. One thing was for sure TK didn't drive them home!

TK and caravan duly arrived at The Dew Drop Inn early on Friday evening before the clay shooting competition the following day. He pulled onto the village green front car park and made the customary entrance to the pub to request permission for the overnight stay.

He was good for business and there was no way I would refuse the man's earlier request. As was also customary with TK, he would insist on buying the landlord and landlady a drink for the privilege of using the car park and facilities. His respects duly paid, TK would retire to his caravan to ready himself for the evening drinking session. The dogs were normally put outside to roam about or sit in the back of the antiquated Landrover and watch the world go by. TK would normally make his entrance with his lovely companions shortly before 9.00pm as a rule. He would treat it as his personal introduction to the public, and a performance to remember! His reputation was well known. The majority of people could take TK on face value. Jake and Evil Emma were amongst the few who disliked TK intensely.

Being Friday night, all our regulars were in and the new student residents from up the road. The new Wye College intake had returned the day before. As is customary, the first week is known as 'refreshers week'. The idea that new students could arrive, settle in and get to know the area before the serious study sessions would begin. It would invariably mean rowdy student newcomers coming to vet the place, prior to the Student Union subsidised bar opening after refreshers week. Jim and his wife had vetted their new third year students carefully again. This year there were three girls and one boy sharing the hall of residence, all of whom had been met in the previous year and appeared to be of the responsible variety!

TK was in full flow with Tom, Helen, Rod and Sal at the bar. His two delightful companions and audience were intent on TK's rambling renditions from Romeo and Juliet whilst he progressively got 'tanked up'. It was all very light hearted and good natured.

Sara was running the restaurant as normal whilst Sue and Molly busied themselves in the kitchen. Smurve and I were behind the bar gloating over TK's companions. Trade was brisk for both food and wet sales. We even had customers seeking out our new steak option that evening. On checking with the kitchen Sue was perfectly happy to take the order. The customer was known to Tom and Helen. LaLa was the proprietor of the Chummy seafood stall in Folkestone harbour and had decided to come out with his wife, son and daughter-in-law to check out our steak meal offer. In latter days he became a regular restaurant customer with the family, every six weeks or so.

He was well known in the area and was respected as the 'whelk king'. To look at, you would have thought he was straight off a pirate ship. Large hooped ear rings, a small nose ring and long black tied back hair. His wrinkled and tanned face was witness to years of saltwater being blown in his face whilst harvesting his whelk crop from his secret location.

LaLa and guests had a great time and left more than satisfied with our offerings later that evening.

In the meantime TK had impressed more of our customers and was now recounting his previous experiences of tarmac paving for exiled foreign royalty in this country. I am not sure if anyone actually believed him, but at the least it was very entertaining!

The evening session gradually drew to a natural close. Most of the regulars had heard enough of TK and his ramblings. The man in question was 'escorted' from the premises by his two delightful companions. TK had earned his 'appearance fee' and was ready for his bed. Despite his glamorous attendees, he was neither fit, nor able to perform, or offer service in any way whatsoever. Clearly, sweet dreams and a mother of hangovers were to come!

By 10.30am the following day both our car parks were full. Word had obviously spread regarding the day's clay pigeon shoot. I was amazed at the response. As before, Smurve was left in charge of the bar and Molly had come in early to prepare for a busy lunchtime session. On the early showing, we would not be disappointed. Unfortunately, Jim the reigning champion had been called away on business and was not available to defend his title. At 11.00am sharp enrolment for the shooting competition commenced. Virtually all the previous entrees were there along with visitors from outside of our area. In all there were fifty-four entrants for the competition, a somewhat hung over TK included. Just the remedy for a rampant hang over; 50+ contestants blasting away at clay misfits for pigeons! As in the previous session, I was the 'trapman'. 3 clays were thrown for practice and getting one's eye in. TK was suffering and declined the 'warm-up' offer.

The competition shoot followed with a winner's pot of £110 at stake. From the practice round I realised there were some serious contenders in attendance. The hamlet resident contestants tried hard to compete. As before Rod was on form and the best contender using my loaned Poachers under and over gun. He concluded his round with a very respectable 8 from 10 score.

Two unknown entrants followed with 9 from 10 scores and tied for the lead. That was until TK took his peg. In an apparent drunken stupor he brandished an ancient 410, hammer action side by side dual barrelled shotgun. No matter what combination of clays I launched, TK was ahead of the game. Each pair of clays that were launched, TK hit with a 'clean kill'. Directly hitting and powdering the clay target without any question of doubt of the result. Large and small clays received TK's own brand of treatment! He was a true master of clay pigeon shooting. As a pigeon, one should always remember to steer well clear of TK to survive!

Needless to say, TK was never seriously challenged. His perfect score, and the way he achieved it, was poetry in motion. I awarded him the winner's pot after the competition. He rewarded us by staying on and probably spent the lion's share of his winnings over the bar. We were however, on guard for future competitions. TK was not to be messed with, hungover or sober. A true country bumpkin, born and bred, but with the eye of Dead-Eyed Dick!

The aftermath of the exciting shooting competition was a bit subdued. The desired effect for the lunchtime session had been achieved with good increases in sales in both food and drink as a direct result of the increased attendance. Could the raised local interest be maintained in the knowledge that someone of TL's calibre could be taking part?

The regular event ran up until Christmas. TK never participated again as there were obviously more lucrative opportunities being offered elsewhere. General apathy and lack of interest resulted in a termination of the regular competition early in the New Year that followed. Whilst it lasted, the Clay Pigeon competition served its purpose. Additional business had been generated during the difficult period running up to the busy Christmas and Festive season.

CHAPTER 12 – Heads above water

In a publican's calendar, the months of November and February are undoubtedly the most difficult to weather from a business perspective. November would be a dreary month with few highlights to look forward too. Bonfire night at the beginning of the month could stimulate a little interest although by the time one had taken into account the additional costs of putting on a firework display, most publicans would find themselves out of pocket. The high risk of inclement weather at this time of year could also make the difference between profit and loss. We had discussed the possibilities of putting on a firework display for the punters but on balance decided against it. Our local footfall was too low and our customer base was largely made up of more mature customers who either would not personally appreciate a display, or didn't have access to a tribe of youngsters that might! There was no real commercial advantage to us staging a firework display.

It seemed that we were to be at the mercy of our normal trade only through November until our Christmas trade could kick in.

However, on one visit to the Cash and Carry, Sue had noticed a customer notification that the 1988 Beaujolais Nouveau would be released on the third Thursday in November, the 17th.

This gave her an idea that we both discussed on her return. Historically, the newly produced wine would be released from the vineyards within the Burgundy Beaujolais producing areas in France on the third Thursday in November and 'raced' by the producers to the trendy wine bars and merchants in Paris. In latter years the race destinations have become virtually every capital city in the world. The London leg has seen a true race style develop with competitors entering high powered sports cars to speed the new wine to the final destination in the shortest time possible! It has become an event that can be likened to the London – Monte Carlo Rally but without the prestige or a prize pot at the end. Ideal for wealthy grown boys and their toys to pass the time of day!

Sue thought we could arrange a Beaujolais Nouveau Race and charity themed night to coincide with the new release. It would be themed around the new wine release at which we could lay on a French style running buffet. By introducing a charity theme we may be able to approach our suppliers to seek their support and gain extra promotion in return.

By chance the very successful TV comedy series 'Allo 'Allo was running, giving an obvious theme for the evening and an added opportunity for fancy dress to be worn. My immediate thoughts were very positive. It would certainly be different to what the other pubs in the area would be doing to attract trade. Subject to getting our suppliers support I agreed that it was worth a try.

The following day I rang around and was very surprised at the positive reaction the majority of our suppliers showed towards the charitable event. Allied offered a free keg of Guinness; West Country Products donated three crates of Belgian beer; our wine merchant provided a bottle of champagne as a raffle prize and a bottle of French brandy; Glen sent us half a dozen French Maigret duck breasts and two dozen escargot; the frozen food supplier sent us a case of French patisserie and a classic Paris-Brest dessert. All in all the suppliers generosity was very much appreciated and was of great assistance in the overall cost planning of the event. We posted prominent notices around the pub and restaurant to advertise the up coming Charity and Fancy Dress event. I also booked an eighth page advert in the local paper to further highlight the theme night.

Clearly, the potential to be victims of our own success with this venture were clear. We both hoped that the evening would be popular, primarily for the locals and regulars, but from a commercial angle, like the clay shoot, the offer had to be opened up to appeal to other potential punters to make it a commercial success. With a host of offers to be made on the night, and to distract the 'free-loading' new student intake, we decided entrance would be by ticket only. The price paid would include the free running buffet, an initial raffle ticket entry and a fifty pence donation to charity. The ticket price was set at £3.50 to be reserved in advance or on the door. Locals and regulars would pay £2.50 as an added incentive. Fancy dress wearers were also entered into a separate draw for the bottle of champagne. We were to run special offers on Guinness at £1.00 per pint, of which fifty pence went to charity. The Belgian beer was offered at the special price of £0.50 of which twenty five pence went to charity. The bottle of French brandy was the top raffle prize for all attendees on the night.

Deidre, Molly and Sue were getting their heads around a suitable running buffet with a French theme. Vol-au-vent s with escargot fillings, French cheese savoury pastries, chicken, garlic and mushroom tartlets, French style quiches, Duck and orange canapés were all decided upon.

Most could be prepared in advance and rolled out on the night as an easy finger buffet. Sage butter roasted potato slices and baguette brochettes completed the offering with a selection of cheese and sausages on sticks and snack nibbles. In all we catered for and hoped for 150 guests.

To further enhance the ambience we all decided to attend in fancy dress. I would be Renee, Sue would be Madame Edith, Smurve would be Monsieur Alfonse, Deidre would be Mimi and Molly would be Yvette. All of us got into our respective characters. It was going to be a good night. Nothing could go wrong so we all thought! Historically, since owning The Dew Drop Inn we had become past masters of expecting the un-expected on a lot of occasions. The first weekend in November had followed a very quiet weeks trading. On two nights we had closed early due to the lack of customers. Smurve and I were fed up with playing darts with each other to amuse ourselves, waiting for the customers that didn't appear. There was little else to do. Even the Friday night was unusually quiet and the takings were only a third of what I would normally expect.

The weather may well have been a contributory factor. It was cold, wet and windy virtually all week long. It was the sort of weather that encouraged you to stay in doors.

The day that followed was little different. Like the previous days it was dull, overcast and windy making it a pretty dismal and gloomy picture. Still it was Saturday, 'our busiest day' I told myself 'we've never been let down yet on a Saturday!' I thought optimistically. Show's how wrong you could be. We suffered one of the worst day's trading. Not even a walking party or trip out customer. Everything was so quiet. Deidre, Sara and Molly were twiddling their thumbs. I was seriously worried. Staff wages had to be paid, heating and lighting costs as well. We couldn't sustain these losses for very long. I consulted with Sue and we decided that if no customers appeared by 9.00pm we would close up and send the staff home. Naturally we would have to pay the full shift rate. It wasn't their fault our trade had nosedived, nor ours come to that! I even seriously thought about cancelling the Sunday Roast Lunch to reduce our loss, things were getting that bad.

Sunday morning arrived. Following the lack of business throughout the earlier days of trading I was finding it very difficult to motivate myself to complete the preparations for opening.
No wonder publicans take this time of year to have a holiday! It was so depressing! Locals and regulars seemed to shun us in our hours of need.
All the staff turned up for their shift. Even they seemed to be as down as both Sue and I were. 'A stiff upper lip and soldier on' that's the spirit I kept telling myself even though deep down I knew it was bullshit!
Deidre came in asking under the circumstances, whether to push ahead with the roasts as normal. I took the view that the meat would not be wasted as we would re-process and sell it somehow before it became Roscoe's dinner!
'Yeah, go for it! Beef and Pork, we'll throw caution to the wind!' I instructed.
Smurve had lit the fires, collected more logs and fully stocked the two inglenooks. Even though it was horrible outside, we were 'snug as bugs in a rug' inside.
All the Sunday preparations were complete and the doors were opened at 11.45am.
Again there were no customers in sight. Smurve and I were on our second game of darts.
'This is doing my 'ead in. It's Bloody Chinese torture!' Smurve commented as he threw his arrows. I found it difficult to disagree. I just stepped up to the ochie and threw my darts.
'Twenty bloody six again!' the world was definitely against me I thought. Smurve just laughed.
The door latch lifted and Tom appeared in the doorway.
'Am I glad to see you?' I welcomed him as I went behind the bar.
'Someone shut the ruddy roads off again boy?' Tom asked sarcastically. He knew things were bad and didn't have to rub it in. I placed his English Ale and pot on the bar.
'One for you and Smurve as well' Tom offered whilst stoking up his pipe.
It was Sunday lunchtime and 12.15 with just one customer. Whatever next!
Deidre came out from the kitchen and asked about the bar roast potatoes. I gave her instructions to wait until 12.30. It appeared that our downtime was continuing.

Then completely without any warning, cars started appearing from every direction. From being as dead as the Marie Celeste, we were heaving within a ten minute timeframe. What a relief! I could have kissed every customer as they entered!

I quickly dashed out to the kitchen to warn the girls that we were up and running, big time! I came back to the bar under the impression that the girls thought I was winding them up. Smurve and I were at full tilt. Even if we had six arms each we would have been struggling to keep up with the demand.

Deidre came to the bar with the bar 'freebies', roast potatoes and cheese on sticks as normal. The expression on her face was a picture when she realised I wasn't joking earlier.

Sara was next in line to face the customer 'Tsunami'. The restaurant was filled in absolutely no time whatsoever. Sunday roasts were in seriously heavy demand.

I had to switch places with Sue to help Deidre in the kitchen. Carving was her 'Nemesis' and I had to step in to help. I cut both Beef and Pork joints in half and started to carve everything off as quickly and accurately as possible under the watchful eye of Roscoe whose head was framed within the kitchen window. He knew the unusable scrag ends of each joint would be his later on. He couldn't wait.

Both Molly and Deidre were working in unison, plating up roast meals as fast as they could. Sara would serve them as soon as they were ready. It was a very well oiled machine in operation. Just as well as there was a lot of making up to be done due to the poor performance throughout the week.

I went back to the bar having completed my first stint of carving. It was still packed and people were queuing and waiting for a restaurant table. The AK gang had finally turned in with Bob and Sal for their normal Sunday lunchtime session. The old pub was on song again!

Sue left and went back to assist in the kitchen again. She took with her a few bar food orders for preparation for customers in the bar. Sue and Smurve had struggled to keep up with the demand for drinks in the bar. It really was uncanny how we had been so quiet, but were now really struggling to keep apace with the demand.

By 1.30pm the girls had served 46 roast meals and 12 bar meals. I was called back to the kitchen to carve the second halves of the beef and pork meat joints. On the surface it appeared the demand was pretty even for both. I didn't hang around and carved both joints as quickly as possible. The girls in the meantime had reloaded the vegetable requirements to continue with our busy spell. The early customers were now leaving and were highly complimentary of the meals they had just taken.

Sara was benefiting from the gratuities and tips customers were leaving. It was always a good, re-assuring sign of satisfaction when tips were left.

By the time I returned to the bar it was 1.45pm. There were no obvious signs of the restaurant demand abating. Once a party left the restaurant another took their place. Sara had the common sense to have a 'waiting list'. She constantly checked in the kitchen regarding the availability of the roast meals in particular. The last thing we wanted was to take an order we could not honour.

I was in the throws of serving the AK gang when I heard a familiar voice

'Watcher you old bugger! How's it hanging?' I stopped what I was doing and turned to see the beaming smile of my former business partner Peter, his wife Nan and two children George and Kim. I was temporarily speechless. Smurve saw my predicament and continued with the AK gang round.

'Well I'm blowed! Hi guys how the devil are you all?' I replied as we shook hands. This was the first time I had seen Peter or his family since we had parted company.

'Neal and Grant told me they had been down. We thought we might come out for a spot of lunch.' Peter was always very precise and proper when speaking.

What a time for them all to turn up I thought to myself. They could have come yesterday!

Peter was like me, a keen connoisseur of real ale. He had seen what was on offer and immediately unilaterally elected Nan to do the driving.

'Is all the water passed by the management?' Peter asked. His sense of humour was always as dry and sharp as ever.

'Pint of Harveys I should think old man?' I asked

'But of course' he replied.

'Nan what can I get you and the kids?' I asked

'I'll have an orange juice and lemonade and the kids can have cokes with straws for the children, please.' Nan replied.

I completed serving the order and asked if they were looking for bar food or roast meals.

Roast meals were the preferred option but bar meals would be okay as time was getting on.

I went out to the kitchen to tell Sue of Peter and Nan's visit and checked with Sara how we were progressing in the restaurant.

I added Peter and family to the waiting list. We were already half way through a complete turnover of all the tables in the restaurant. We could accommodate the latest party just within the meat stock availability. I went back to the bar to find Sue had come from the kitchen to welcome our guests.

Peter insisted that the drinks and meals should be paid for and a tab should be opened.

He bought Sue, Smurve and me a drink. That was something of a novelty as in our earlier drinking days Peter would normally be the last to put his hand in his pocket!

It really was refreshing to see the whole family again.

Time had moved on to shortly before 2.15pm when Peter and family were accommodated in the restaurant. Deidre and Molly were in the last throws of their meal service. I took them out a drink and asked how things had gone. They were quite buoyant and showed me how much meat was left. I explained the last order was for a special guest so for the adult meals lay it on a bit thicker than normal. I said all would be revealed in due course as I was certain Peter was there to stay all afternoon and probably into the evening session. I knew my ex- business partner very well and sure enough my assumption was spot on.

The lunchtime bar session inevitably had to overrun. We had so much ground to make up from the earlier week we needed all we could get. All the time we had restaurant diners there was little point in closing the bar. Even the AK gang were showing signs of reluctance to leave. Jim was in a rare and generous mood and was buying Glenfidich malt whiskies for his party. The horrible weather clearly had its benefits!

With the exception of Peter and his family the last remaining restaurant diners left shortly after 3.40pm. The kitchen staff members had excelled themselves and were well into the winding down and clear up operation. They finished everything by 4.00pm as had Smurve and me in the bar. We had closed up and decided to have a relaxing wind down drink in the bar together with Peter and

Nan. It was great catching up. Peter was obviously continuing to do well with our former business. This confirmed what I had gleaned from Neal and Grant from their earlier visits.

Both Peter and Nan loved our pub. They felt the history, age and olde worlde charm of the place was wonderful. The real ale selection was nothing short of heaven for Peter.

By the time we sat down with them, he had already tried three of the ales. The 'piece de resistance' Old Thumper was saved to last along with my little anecdote to tell. Peter was most impressed with our abilities to look after and serve a beautiful array of ales.

Kim and George went out with Amanda and Kate to play on the activity tree and to meet Roscoe for the first time. Everyone got on famously – it was just like old times.

Time just flew by and Smurve had returned for the evening session, opening the doors at 7.00pm. Peter had made a strange request. He had never worked behind a bar before and wondered if I would object to him 'taking the reigns' for a couple of hours. It was an ideal opportunity for Sue and Nan to catch up so I took the kitchen duty, which enabled me to be out front in the bar, customer side, leaving Peter to play. Funnily enough Peter was a natural mine host. He was very welcoming, impeccably polite and reasonably proficient behind the bar. It was a novelty for the local and regular Sunday night customers as well. Peter loved it and would have stayed to closing time if he could. The children were getting tired and Nan had decided it was time to bring Peter back to earth and head for home. We bade our farewells and agreed to meet up again later in the year. It was a normal Sunday night trade with a few bar meals and the usual customers in.

Running our business in the days that followed was proving a little tedious. We were rarely busy and more than likely, losing money. It was however to be expected due to the general apathy of the public at that time of year. We had pinned our hopes on having a special charity theme night a few days later.

Right on cue the local paper was published with our feature advertisement. Initially, we had a considerable number of telephone enquiries regarding the event. Everything appeared to be coming together nicely.

Deidre had agreed to come in the evening before and after she finished her normal work on the day of the event. Molly had been primed by Sue what had to be done and during the quieter lunchtime sessions a lot of preparations could be made for the running buffet. The weather had turned colder with night frosts but sunny by day. At least the rain appeared to have subsided for the time being.

All the suppliers had stood by their offers of support and provided their agreed products.

Costumes had been made and everything was up to speed. Sue had been to the wine merchants and collected our stock of the new seasons Beaujolais Nouveau which we would offer for sale to the customers by the bottle or by the glass.

Sue collected Deidre as pre-arranged, after finishing her normal shift and headed up to the pub. There was little time to lose.

Smurve and Molly stayed over between sessions to help out. I had acquired some red white and blue ribbon tape to drape around the bar and Syd had somehow acquired and loaned us a couple of French national flags that could also be used to embellish the bar. Candle lights were put on all the tables to give that extra authentic bistro effect. It really was a good transformation. Phone calls were still being received for instructions how to find us, and the entry times. Everything was prepared and completed by 5.00pm.

Calamity struck! Shortly before 5.00pm, as darkness rolled in, so did the fog. The thickest 'pea soup' fog you can imagine. I don't think I have ever experienced any fog thicker than that night. It was so thick that even our floodlights could not penetrate it! Clearly unless it lifted quickly, no one would attempt to drive out to our event. To do so would have been too risky to say the least. It was soul destroying and so dis-heartening. However, one had to stay positive. There was an hour and a half before things got under way. There was nothing for us to do other than hope the wind might get up and clear the air.

Seven o'clock came and the fog remained as thick as ever, maybe even thicker. What ever could we do? We were all sat around in fancy dress waiting and hoping the weather would be kind and clear the fog. Unfortunately it didn't. What an absolute nightmare!

The cruellest twist of fate was still to come. At about 9.15pm a light breeze built up and cleared the fog away leaving the clearest moonlit night you could imagine. The reprieve from the fog was obviously too late to attract ticket paying customers as over half of the session had gone. Clive had been working late and popped in for a drink on the way home. He was our first customer and that was about 9.20pm.

Mark and Gordon came up from Wye, expecting to find the place alive for the advertised event. They couldn't believe what had happened. Ironically, even our stalwart locals didn't come out!

It was most certainly the biggest disappointment and worst financial disaster we had experienced in the whole history of owning The Dew Drop Inn. It was a massive pill to have to swallow. Never again would we try anything so ambitious.

The whole event was a complete washout. In total, we had six customers turn up in the whole session, three of whom were family members who came from Folkestone to support the event. The fog had admittedly delayed them, but they finally arrived at 9.25pm. Those present were invited to enjoy the buffet and takeaway as much as they liked. There was way too much to even consider freezing it all. The Sunday lunch 'freebies' were definitely going to be different this week for sure! I invited the staff to take home what they wanted. They were just as sick about the event as we were. The last thing on their minds was to take the food home. I decided, rather than throw the surplus food away I would bag up what was perishable and send it up to Lorna to feed to the pigs. She was very grateful, as were the pigs. They were probably the only satisfied parties who benefited from our Special event!

CHAPTER 13 – On song again

The extreme disappointment of our earlier theme night took time to get over. It was all too easy to look for someone, or something to blame for its failure. Hard and unpalatable as it seemed, one could only really blame bad luck. Had the fog not been there the chances are it would have been a great success. No one would know for sure. The only thing we had to do was put the matter behind us and move on. On a more positive note, we were in the final days of November and the run up to Christmas was not far away.

Sue and I had discussed what options we could consider for the festive season. In the licensed trade the Christmas season starts from 1st December. Pubs are normally decked out in their Christmas decorations and finery by then, to capitalise on the increase in trade. Special meals and festive fayre are put on to attract more trade. Office parties can be lucrative affairs and should be encouraged where possible.

We asked Glen to pop in and advise what seemed to be 'hot' in the trade that year. He gave us some good indicators and ideas of how to be that little bit different. It seemed that 3 bird roasts were topping the bill for this Christmas. A 3 bird roast reputedly dates back to medieval times. A turkey or goose is stuffed with a chicken, which has been stuffed with a duck. In reality, today the various birds are 'butterfly boned' and then rolled together giving a joint that is easy to cook and carve. The three meats are distinguishable after carving and plating up. Nice if you like that sort of thing!

For our part, we decided to keep traditional and as simple as possible. 'Butterfly boned' turkey joints with inner stuffing were our favoured option. Cooking was straight forward, carving was easy and on the plate it looked terrific with each slice having a heart shaped core of stuffing. All the trimmings were to be provided. Glen had provided us with a terrific price for the meat and advised that this method could also be re-heated in an autoclave or combination oven which made it all the more entertaining. This meant that we could actually offer the Christmas menu option for walk in trade as well. Cold turkey salads and sandwiches were also introduced in addition to avoid meat wastage. This would be in addition to the ever popular steaks and existing bar and special's menus.

We thought long and hard about whether to offer a Christmas Day Lunch. Undeniably a major profit spinner, but the extra staffing cost, commitment, unreliability aspects of both customers and part-time junior staff put us off. We decided the bar would open for drinks and snacks only for the lunchtime session, closing at 3.00pm sharp so we too could enjoy our Christmas with the children. I decided that we would also stand every customer their first drink on the day as an added attraction to those who ventured out. Sue had suggested free mince pies may go down well in addition. We had finally agreed our Christmas timetable and menu strategy.

All we had to do now was find the customers and staff to cook and serve.

First up Deidre and Molly were approached. Deidre had to be counted out for lunchtime sessions until the 19th. December, after the schools broke up. She was happy to work any other evenings as required. Molly was happy to work most shifts with notice.

Smurve just took everything in his stride and was happy to work when needed. Sara was attending Kent University at Canterbury and was living at home. She too was happy to work as and when required with notice.

The plan for our Christmas campaign was complete. All we needed now was to get it underway.

I must submit to being a self-confessed Scrooge and Humbug at Christmas. Much to my own family's disgust, I find it very difficult to get into the festive spirit nowadays. However, this year the challenge was that much greater, as the business was counting on a successful campaign to get back on track following the disastrous November we had just been through.

In the closing days of November, Sue had been to Cash and Carry to load up on every conceivable type of decoration available. Tree, table, ceiling decorations you name it, Sue found it! For my part, I went off to see Malcolm in Hothfield again. Rumour had it he supplied the best Christmas trees in the area. The rumours were in fact completely true. I purchased two seven foot high, beautiful Norwegian spruce Christmas trees from him. As a past good customer he only charged me £12 for both trees. Unbeknown to me Malcolm had been up to the pub on two separate occasions, since delivering the beer garden furniture.

I didn't recall him being there, but his rantings over our real ales, Old Thumper in particular, proved he must have been there.

I suggested he should return and let me reciprocate his generosity with a pint on the house.

Half an hour later, I was back at the pub setting my trees in buckets of shingle for siting in the bar and restaurant. Sue and I agreed the lower bar door would be shut off and an ideal position for the bar tree. The restaurant was placed in the lounge area corner beside the fireplace. Sue set about decorating the trees with Molly's help. Clearly both women enjoyed the Christmas spirit. I just let them get on with it. I had done my bit I thought!

By the time the girls came out of school the Christmas decorations in the bar were up and the trees completed. The women I must confess had done a really good job. Even logs in the fireplaces had been sprayed with imitation snow for effect. Yet another triumph of a 'mini makeover' had been performed.

Both our daughters' eyes lit up the minute they came in from school. It really was a pleasure to see. Even Roscoe gave his bark of approval to the transformation on seeing it. Things were looking up again.

I took a telephone call the following morning from a gentleman stating he was the Master of the East Kent Hunt. He explained it was the policy of his members to seek out different welcoming hostelries in their area with the facilities to accommodate a Hunt meet. Would I be interested in seeking their patronage? The East Kent Hunt would normally meet mid week during the hunting season. The next date proposed was the first Wednesday in December. It was extremely short notice I thought but felt it could only be advantageous for the business. The Master did explain the police would be in force to control the proceedings as saboteurs were now commonplace, intent on upsetting the smooth running of the hunt. I had no feelings either way. I could understand the cruelty argument, but also appreciated the damage that foxes could cause in the countryside. I don't know for sure how many foxes were actually caught by hunting. Far more were casualties of 'lamping', the process of nocturnal hunting and shooting the prey when dazzled by a spotlight. At least with the hunt the wily fox did stand a chance of out running the hounds and riders and getting away! I was delighted to accept the Masters request and looked forward to seeing the Hunt a couple of days later. As was traditional the hounds would arrive first, followed by the horses and their riders. Ponies and their junior riders would be the last to arrive. I gather this gave the 'gentry' time to consume enough cherry brandy and whiskey-mac to muster up sufficient Dutch courage to take up the chase!

I told Sue about the Hunt's up and coming visit, explaining that the police would be in attendance should the saboteurs get a little out of hand. Apparently, the pub used to be a regular meeting point for the hunt years ago. They hadn't been back for some years because the area had become so congested with horse boxes, followers and saboteurs. I am led to believe our new car park and the recent improvements we had made at the pub had put us back on the map as a possible Meet venue.

The Wednesday was soon on us. It was an overcast, cold morning but at least it was dry. Pc Stone our local policeman was the first to arrive at the pub with another two of his colleagues in their patrol cars. An additional support minibus followed to be in reserve with another ten policemen. They all came in for a gratefully received coffee and bacon rolls. They explained their normal procedure would be to block off the access roads to all but members of the hunt fraternity. The three patrol cars left after finishing their coffee to set up the road blocks.

The hounds didn't actually have to come that far. They were kennelled on the top of the North Downs above Wye and it was easier to walk them with their kennel staff up to the pub. They looked a picture coming up the hill in front of the pub. The leading hound's man was dressed in white jodhpurs, black boots and sported a green riding jacket and riding hat and walked ahead of the hounds. He carried a whip in one hand and a small hunting horn, he periodically blew, to keep the following pack of excited hounds moving.

The East Kent Hunt members were all well known to the police, and in the main were highly respected members of the community. They were the next to arrive. A circuit Judge, accountants, lawyers, doctors and executive businessmen and women belonged to the select and prestigious organisation. Each rider had their own horsebox and valet in attendance. The junior members were last to arrive with their ponies in horseboxes.

There were also quite a number of supporters of the hunt on foot. They were members of the public who had an interest in supporting and following hunting, but not actively taking part in the proceedings. It was a healthy activity, out in the fresh air and quite a spectacle to boot.

Hunt saboteurs trying to disrupt the proceedings were initially stopped well short of the meeting place and instructed to move on by

the duty policeman. Invariably they had to find alternative parking places and come on foot, normally across the fields to the pub. Once at the pub, the on site policemen ensured the saboteurs were restrained and separated from the supporters. There was a little banter and remonstration between the parties but little else. In the main, things were pretty well managed and good natured.
On the other hand, inside the bar, cherry brandy and whiskey mac was being sunk like no tomorrow. I was surprised to note the age of most of the participants. I had naturally met the Master of the Hunt who must have been in his mid sixties. He had the honour of course of being dressed 'in the pink'. His scarlet tunic and hunting horn were the symbols of his authority and office. He thanked me for the use of the facilities and had assured me the Hunt account would be settled on his return. In the meantime everyone dressed in hunt regalia should be served with what they wanted and charged to his account. Money would not change hands! Furthermore, he asked for trays of sherry and cherry brandy to be offered to the riders once mounted, to toast the fox and the hunt just before the 'off'.
There were two elderly gentlemen in the bar totally wrapped up in the event and enjoying every second of it. One must have been in his early seventies, his companion nearer eighty. They had been seriously drinking and recounting their hunt adventures to Smurve. They just loved the old pub and its surroundings, the Whiskey Mac's and the cherry brandy even more.
The Master of the Hunt blew his horn as an order to 'mount up'. It was also the sign for Smurve and me to ready the trays of drinks to offer to the riders once mounted up.
The two elderly gents in the bar finished their drinks and amidst mutterings of 'duty calls' struggled to their feet, stood swaying about and donned their black velvet tunics, collected their riding hats and crops and gingerly staggered to the door.
'How the 'ell are they going to ride a bloody horse like that?' Smurve muttered to me under his breath.
'Christ knows!' I replied.
The older gentleman headed towards his mount. It was a fabulous 16.5 hand chestnut hunter horse with white 'boots'. His valet had prepared the horse to perfection. Its plaited main and matching tail with a brushed coat that positively glistened was a picture to see. Even better, the valet provided a special mounting block for his 'master' to get on to the horse. His saddle was something else. It was

virtually a cradle for the rider to sit in, not on, leaving the horse to follow the hunt, taking the rider, not vice versa.

The spectacle was even better now than ever. I went out and round the riders with a tray of hot mince pies. As it was Christmas I thought it would be a nice gesture. There were some takers but not many. So as not to waste any returned pies I thought it would be a nice gesture to offer the remaining pies to the onlookers.

Whoops! Guess who mistook saboteurs for supporting onlookers? 'Oh well, such is life!' I thought to myself and hurriedly returned to the bar.

By the time I had returned, Smurve had duly prepared the sherry and cherry brandy trays. We collected them and went outside.

All the riders were now mounted. The Master called the proceedings to order and removed his riding hat, bowing his head. All the other riders dutifully followed their leader's actions. The Master said a short prayer, finished with a collective 'Amen' and replaced his riding hat. He gave us the nod to offer the drink selection to all the horse riders. The pony riders just stood and looked on. The Master duly toasted the Fox and the Hunt and knocked back his cherry brandy in one. Smurve and I collected the glasses as quickly as we could. The Master raised his horn to his mouth and blew the customary 'Come on Down' rallying call. The hounds immediately picked up on the sound of the horn. With a loud crack of the Masters whip, the East Kent Hunt moved of in search of their sport.

The hunt was soon out of sight with only the occasional horn blow and barking of the chasing pack decipherable across the valley.

What a wonderful experience and privilege we had hosting the Hunt. An old country tradition of the past as traditional fox hunting has now been outlawed.

My biggest regret of the whole hunt episode was not having a camera on hand to record the colour and spectacle at the pub. The various tunic colours, the horses and hounds, riders on horseback contrasting with our lovely old pub setting was second to none. It was an absolute delight to witness, even my minor transgression with the saboteurs.

The hunt duly returned about two hours later. All the riders attested to a good ride and fine sport. They didn't actually catch anything. The fox, if there was one outsmarted the hounds and their following riders. The riders dismounted and the valets led the steaming horses away to their boxes in preparation for their journey home. The riders in the main left with their mounts with the exception of the Master and the two senior gentlemen in the pub earlier. I was formally introduced to the older men as they were former Masters of the hunt. Clearly the fun of the chase had got to all three of them. They rapidly sank three Whiskey Macs each. The reigning Master asked for the bill to pay his dues. I hit the total key on the till to get the final figure of the drinks total. Smurve saw the figure and winced. The Master looked at the receipt. £439.75 was the figure.

'Less than the last one. You're losing your touch boys!' he jokingly taunted his companions. He took out a cheque book and duly wrote out the settlement cheque in favour of The Dew Drop Inn in the sum of £500.00.

'I trust we would be welcomed back?' he asked as he handed me the cheque.

'But of course!' I replied 'Very generous. Thank you very much' I continued, having seen the cheque amount.

I duly wrote a receipt, handed it to the Master, shook hands and he left with his Hunt colleagues.

'With business like that, come everyday!' I mused to Smurve.

The last of the horseboxes had pulled away as the first of the day's customers pulled up for lunch. It had been a memorable day so far. The Christmas season was quickly getting into gear. The whole ambience of the pub had been lifted as well as our trade level and takings, thank goodness! Every trading session was now being well attended. Our Christmas meals were going down well with the customers. We had introduced a daily curry lunch alternative for those people who were already fed up with turkey as happens at this time of year. Our standard bar menu was also available for the lighter meal option to cater for the smaller appetite. I believe we had the balance spot on to cover virtually all our customer's needs. The bar sales of drinks were also well ahead. The real ale selection was tweaked for the festive season. I temporarily dropped the Fullers London Pride in favour of appropriately named Humbug ale from the Marston's brewery. A darker, stronger bitter beer produced for the Christmas market.

As was the norm, West Country Products supplied us with their customary buy two, get one free offer. The beer's promotional pump clip was a masterpiece. The classic Santa Claus image re-modelled into Scrooge. Customers were electing to try the beer, purely on sight of the novelty beer clip alone!

It is quite amazing how time just flies by when you are busy. Bookings and events throughout December come and go so quickly, you even question in your own mind whether they really did happen. The visit of the East Kent Hunt was one such event. It was memorable, of course, but was over before it had almost started. The local village school next door to us were staging events in the lead up to Christmas. The school only had a role of twenty-four pupils, two of whom were our daughters. Unlike larger schools, the reduced numbers of pupils meant any productions put on would probably require full participation of the whole school. The Christmas nativity play was no exception. Both our girls had their designated parts to play. Amanda the eldest had the part of a wise man, Kate was the angel Gabrielle.

The penultimate week of the Christmas school term was dedicated to rehearsing and perfecting the production, culminating in three evening presentations for parents, relatives and friends alike to attend. The presentations were timed to start at 7.00pm and to be completed by 8.00pm. This was good and bad for business. On the downside the village green parking would be filled up early before we opened. Luckily our new rear parking facility accommodated the early overspill demand without materially affecting our trade. On the upside, by the time the production had finished and people were starting to leave, the pub would be at its most enticing. Most people were upbeat having just seen their little darling's performance and a quick drink, or two to celebrate, was very much in order. The three production nights were most welcomed from the business angle!

The final day of the week at school was a reward day. The school Christmas Party had been arranged. The kitchen cooks were providing a traditional lunch of their own with Turkey and Christmas pudding for all. The afternoon session was set aside for games in the school hall, culminating with a carol service and the customary visit from Santa Claus to meet the children and distribute presents. Parents were invited to attend the Carol Service and see Santa for themselves.

For our part, Friday was always a hectic day regardless of the fact it was Christmas time as well. The restaurant had a lunchtime block booking from Quest International for their Sales and Admin Department. Quest is a local manufacturer of perfumes and similar based products in Ashford. Their booking was for forty guests, all having the set Christmas lunch menu option. Molly and Sue had their work cut out in the kitchen with this function alone. Conveniently, Sara had finished at university for the Christmas recess earlier in the week and was available to waitress service for the Quest function. We were confident of still getting our normal fair share of walk-in trade on top of the Quest function as well. Things were going to be extremely busy again.

Smurve and I had the pipe cleaning and bar preparation to contend with and dray visits from Allied and West Country Products. The brewery trade would generally respond to the increased demand by offering additional deliveries throughout December. We took advantage of these as our stockholding capability was limited, and at the busiest times one could run the risk of running out of beer, god forbid!

We were ready and open exactly on time at noon. In theory the Quest party was due to arrive at 12.15 for a 12.30pm sit down. The 'on the road' sales representatives were a lot cuter than most. They had made arrangements to meet earlier and were with us very shortly after opening. The party of six salespeople were ahead of the others. Five very attractive females and the sole male representative were impeccably dressed, as one would expect from professional sales people. White wine Spritzers were selected by all the women, their male colleague indulged in a pint of Humbug. His selection of Humbug left him wide open to the females ridiculing him mercilessly. It was all harmless fun, for the women at least! I wondered if the unfortunate salesman would dare to have another Humbug later on. Despite his 'sufferings' he enjoyed the beer immensely. As he was not driving he did indeed partake in another Humbug later on.

The rest of the Quest party followed on as arranged. The company had hired a coach for the visit, which meant no–one really needed to worry about drink driving. The party were all in party mood and brought the place alive in no time. Like the Hunt booking, I was told Quest would be settling the bill. An itemised bill would need to be submitted for all food and drinks. The Sales Director greeted me and gave me a confirmation Purchase Order for the function.

Smurve and I went into action serving as quickly as possible.
As anticipated, when 'free' beer is on offer guests were inclined to get carried away. I told Smurve to use a little discretion with the guests. Spirit measures should be limited to doubles. I didn't feel Quest would want to see anything on their bill other than standard or

large measure descriptions. Of course we both knew that two large whiskies were probably poured in to one on leaving the bar. At least we felt we were seen to be trying to control the situation!

Despite the heavy drinking, the Quest event went off very well. The girls in the kitchen and restaurant coped admirably. As predicted, we had a further forty to fifty customers through the bar for drinks and snack lunches.

Unusually, one pair of male customers were completely dis-satisfied with the service we offered, and left vowing never to return after just one drink, and they left most of that. I was a little gob smacked by their reaction to me, being unable to take their food order for two steak and kidney pies, chips and peas. We didn't, and never had offered pies and chips on our bar menu.

'All bloody pubs do steak and kidney pie and chips! If they don't they ain't a good pub!' I was told in no uncertain terms.

I re-iterated my apology and asked if they might prefer something else, only to be given a foul mouthed response from both of them in return. I had never been spoken to like that in all the time we had been at the pub. My temper was roused and I wasn't feeling 'goodwill to all men', particularly those two ignoramus'. I was fired up and ready to fight! The bar occupants watched in horror as the incident unfolded in front of them. As they left I tried to breathe deeply to calm down and relax a little. The bar had gone quiet.

Having composed myself I offered a general apology to all the customers at what they had just witnessed. I was still upset and annoyed at what had happened. The customers in the bar burst into spontaneous applause for me. Clearly they didn't hold me in any way responsible for what had happened.

Smurve had played a major part in restraining me at the height of the incident, and then calmly told me to ignore them. I had never seen them before. Smurve assured me he knew of them from previous trouble he had witnessed at the Five Bells. Apparently, on that occasion Hans took a different line to me. He told them to leave, escorting them off the premises! I concluded the matter by giving strict instructions should they ever return, they were to be refused service of any sort, and told to immediately leave the premises.

Luckily, our party guests from Quest were totally oblivious to the earlier incident. They had enjoyed themselves and their coach had returned to take them back to Ashford. Whether they were returning to work was another matter entirely! The last to leave was the Sales

Director who thanked me very much for the hospitality, instructing a drink for all the staff should be added to the bill with a £25 itemised gratuity. I shook hands and thanked him for the business as he left. The bar was still busy and I got Smurve to pull me a pint of Old Thumper on Quest's account. He went next door quickly to tell the girls about the drink that were 'in the wood' for them.

I was sat on the bar stool enjoying my beer when the door opened and in rushed Janet, Tom's sister and the school caretaker from next door. She was very flustered and agitated.

'Hiya Janet. It's unusual to see you at this time of day. Is there anything wrong?' I asked.

'Santa's gone sick! We've got no Santa for the kiddiewinks party!' Janet explained

She went on 'Mister Oliver can't do it. The children will recognise him immediately!'

'Calm down. Get your breath back and have a drink. Smurve, get Janet a drink please' I suggested.

'There must be someone else, surely. Where's Mike?' I asked

'He's out delivering to London. He can't do it. Thanks Smurve.' Janet took the coke and had a sip.

Just at that moment Sue came into the bar. Seeing Janet, and the state she had got herself into she asked if everything was okay.

'Santa's gone sick!' I reaffirmed what had already been said.

I took another big long draw on my Old Thumper. I had a very strange feeling I knew what was coming next.

Smurve had become very scarce, away in the cellar on the pretext of checking the spear levels. He was conspicuous by his absence!

'Oh, is that all' Sue said. 'Pat will do it, won't you? It's for the kids!' I wasn't given a chance to answer. It was a 'fait a complete' I had decided. Janet was visibly relieved.

'Oh thanks Pat. Thanks very much. Say 3.30 in the school hall. The costume's in the store room behind.' Janet finished her Coke and hurriedly left the pub.

'Thanks a million! That's just what I need!' I said to Sue. 'Smurve, refill please I'm going to need it!'

Our last customers had left the pub shortly after 3.00pm. I had this sickening feeling in the pit of my stomach thinking about what was to come. I had never done anything like this before and was not looking forward to it one little bit.

Smurve wound me up a little more by going about his bar work humming 'Jingle Bells', interspersed with the odd 'Ho, Ho, Ho!'. As requested I arrived at the school just before 3.30pm. The carol service was in session and due to end within five minutes. Janet met me and took me through to the store room. The Santa costume was on a hanger in all its glory. Janet provided me with extra cushioning to pad me out for the 'portly' effect. As it happened the costume fitted me pretty well over all of the attached padding. Luckily, I had remembered to take my black wellington boots. My shoes would have been an immediate 'give-away' of my identity. I fitted the false beard over my own and pulled up the attached hood, slung the sack of presents over my shoulder and presented myself to Janet for her opinion. She gave me the brass school bell to ring at the right time to announce my arrival. She was delighted! Janet said I was the most realistic Santa the school had seen in years. It made me feel good but did little for my nerves. I was still petrified. The last carol had finished and James Hume, our local vicar, concluded the proceedings with the final prayers. I had left the store room and gone into the playground immediately outside the school hall. Right on cue I started ringing the handbell and interspersed it with cries of 'Yo,ho,ho – Merry Christmas!' After the third rendition the Hall doors were opened revealing all the children sat on the floor with their parents looking on. The realisation that Santa had arrived showed on all their faces. My part was totally un-rehearsed and had to be ad-libbed throughout. I went into the hall waving and 'yo-ho-hoing' all the time. The children could hardly contain their excitement. I was becoming a little more relaxed about my performance and started to become a little more adventurous.
'Has anybody got any carrots for my reindeer Rudolph, please?' I asked
'My reindeer loves his carrots, like I love my glass of sherry and mince pies, you know?' I went on.
I had a totally captivated audience. The children were absolutely mesmerised. Parents were similarly confused and were trying to figure out who was in the suit.
'Now children - Santa likes his carols. Who knows Silent Night?'
'We do!' The kids were keen to respond.
'Are you sure you do?' I said, getting in to pantomime mode.
'Yes we do!' They replied.

'Alright, let's hear it then'. I put the sack down and went into conducting mode. Totally unaccompanied the children gave me their rendition. It was brilliant.
'Oh! So you do know it! That was lovely.' I complimented them.
'Who would like their presents?' I shouted out.
'We do!' the kids responded again.
'Have you all been good boys and girls this year?' I asked
'Yes we have!' they replied.
'Are you really sure?' I questioned
'Yes we have!' they responded in complete unison.
'Alright then, let Santa find a chair and look in his sack'.
I found the nearest chair and sat down. I then opened the sack and took out a present, checked the label and called out the name written on it. The child in question would be beckoned to come and sit on my knee, tell me a little about themselves, collect their present, thank me and wish me a happy Christmas.
I think my action took everyone by surprise. I went through the same procedure for all the children in the school. The parents loved it! Having finished distributing the presents I got back to my feet rang the bell a few times offered a few 'Happy Christmas'' and 'Ho-ho-ho's' and left the hall.
Janet met me outside with tears running down her face.
'Bravo, what a performance! Thanks so much again!'
I went into the back store room to get dis-robed. Mr. Oliver the headmaster popped his head round the door and thanked me for assisting.
I headed quickly back to the pub. I was surprised to find Smurve was still there in the bar.
'Had to wait and see Santa's return!' he taunted me.
'Bollocks!' I replied
'Want a drink?' I asked him.
'Go on. I'll have a pint. I can't be bothered to go home. I'll have to come back as soon as I got there!' Smurve said as I poured his pint.
'Seriously, how did it go?' he asked.
'As it happens it was great!' I replied as I settled down to another pint of Old Thumper.
Just shortly afterwards Kate and Amanda came in from school. Kate was full of herself and eager to tell us about the encounter with Santa Claus. She was young and still a firm believer in Santa Claus.

Smurve and I just sat there and listened to Kate's excited recount of the recent meeting.

'You go and tell Mum all about it.' I said to her. Kate didn't need to be told twice.

Amanda, being the eldest daughter was less enthusiastic.

'So what have you been up to today then Dad?' she asked quizzically.

'Oh been busy here haven't we Smurve?' I replied as Smurve nodded his agreement.

'Funny that. Do you know Father Christmas has got a gingery coloured beard under his big white one? It's just like yours as well! He's also got the same watch as you too! ' Amanda concluded in a very smug fashion.

'Well fancy that!' I replied not intending to continue the conversation. Amanda had obviously rumbled Santa's identity.

As the days of December passed by, Christmas was coming ever nearer. The constant high level of trade was nice to have, even though it was exhausting for all of us. On looking back, I would hate to venture a guess at the number of times I recall having to put on a brave face and give the impression life was such a ball, when secretly all I wanted to do was get away or simply go to bed. There was no let up from the continual pressures of running the business, providing constant customer satisfaction. The art of disguising ones feelings under such conditions were part and parcel of the 'professionalism' modern landlords are required to master.

For our part we were finding less time for ourselves and the family at this time of year. It was a unique experience for both of us. Something as mundane as Christmas shopping was virtually impossible unless it could be incorporated with the regular Cash and Carry visits. Understandably, tensions were created as a result between the good lady and me. We really tried very hard to contain our differences and made every effort to keep them behind closed doors.

Unfortunately, some people consider Christmas time to be an open-season for unruly behaviour and drinking excessively, without a care, or concern for their fellow beings.

A minority of our Wye students were a classic example.

We took a restaurant booking for a combined netball and football function for the end of term. It was on the Tuesday night before their recess.

Forty-two students were to attend the function for our set Christmas meal in the restaurant that we reserved exclusively for them. They wished to dine early which suited us well, so I thought.

The party arrived right on opening and went directly into the bar and started drinking our real ales along with various other strange concoctions. It was clear to see from their reactions that mischief was in the air for some of them. I became aware that some students had brought their own spirits with them, vodka in the main, and were blatantly consuming them on our premises. When initially asked to refrain from the practice they appeared to oblige. The meal was duly served. I had hoped a little sustenance might have a sobering effect. If it did, it was pretty short lived! A very small minority found it amusing to throw the odd brussel sprout at someone else on another table. One thing led to another, before long a virtual 'full-on' food fight was in hand. It was a total disgrace to see, let alone to have to deal with. The majority of the party I am sure were well mannered students looking to have a pleasant evening out. It goes to show how the inconsiderate actions of the minority, are suddenly overtaken in a ground swell of the majority, and respectability and decent behaviour quickly breaks down. The four main perpetrators were identified, as one and the same Vodka secretors, who were duly asked to leave. They were clearly very drunk and must have been drinking well before they had even come to the pub.

Initially they refused to go. At the second time of asking they offered feeble apologies and were still reluctant to leave. On my third and final request, whilst holding the telephone to call for police backup, the offending four got up to leave. Foul language and obscene gesticulations were directed at me as the four left. At the door I advised them they were formally barred from the premises, and they should never return.

On my return to the restaurant the organiser approached me and offered his sincere apology for the earlier incidents. All the female students had set about trying to clear up the mess from the food fight. I accepted their apology and agreed not to take the matter further. The rest of the evening passed off in good vein without any further incidents. They spent well in the end, but the whole incident had left a sour taste in our mouths after they left. It was to be the first and last large booking I would accept from our Wye college students. Once was definitely enough!

Three days before Christmas Eve and the mood changed dramatically. The pub was situated on some of the highest ground in Kent. Christmas Day that year was on a Sunday. It was now Wednesday, as we woke up to the first snow of the winter. Not a lot but a covering of a couple of inches. It was still snowing but very lightly. Were we to have a 'white' Christmas one asked? It was all very exciting. The girls loved it. School had broken up the day before, so the snow couldn't have come at a better time. They played outside in the snow with Mark and Jody, Molly's two children for all the morning.

I initially loved the change in scenery, but I had become a little concerned about the impact the snow covering would have on the business. We had a lot of bookings right up to Christmas Eve. The last thing we wanted, or could afford was another weather derived crisis like we experienced in mid-November.

Smurve had made the journey up from his home in Smeeth. He said the snow was only on the high ground. He encountered it halfway up the face of the North Downs and didn't think it would last, or give us any serious problems. Just to be sure I checked the local weather forecast that indicated the snow would subside by early afternoon and a rapid thaw would set in. So much for a 'white' Christmas, it was nice while it lasted though.

The final lead up to Christmas was as busy as could be expected. Christmas Eve had an extension to normal drinking hours for both sessions.

Christmas Eve was a clear, cold and sunny day. There had been a heavy frost overnight which hardly lifted all day. For my part I left Smurve to do the entire bar preparation, as I had a 'mercy' mission of my own to make into town. I had to collect the girls combined 'big' Christmas present and make the mandatory jewellers visit for her ladyship's special Christmas gift. Folkestone was the best bet for me and would probably be quieter and easier to get in and out of. I headed off early to beat the traffic and crowds.

I collected the girl's Scalectrix racing car set from the high street toy shop that Sue had ordered it from and headed towards the collection of jewellers at the top end of the High Street. As I past one of my favourite outfitters, I marvelled at the caps and hats in the window. As a country boy, I seemed I was lacking something. The hat was obviously what was missing.

I was taken with the deer stalker and traditional country cap in the window. I went in and treated myself to a tweed country cap. A Happy Christmas to me!

A lovely gold bracelet and a couple of gold charms later I was ready to head for home. Not bad going as it was barely 10.00am!

I arrived back at the pub and left the massive box of the Scalectrix and the jewellery in the boot of the car, out of sight, and went in via the back door. I was met outside by Sue who saw the new cap on my head with my leather blouson jacket and burst out laughing, asking me if I thought I was 'Dell-boy' from the comedy series 'Only Fools and Horses'.

I was not amused initially, but on looking in the mirror behind the bar I could see what she meant. Regardless of the mockery, I still liked the tweed cap I had bought for myself earlier!

Smurve had done most things ready to open up. It was going to be a long day and night requiring a lot of stamina and energy for all of us. As we were slightly ahead of time we opened at 11.30am. Tom was the first customer in. He took his rightful place at the bar, offered compliments of the season and offered Smurve and myself a drink as well.

'Bloody cold out there boys! Still, it's lucky the old white stuff came and went, eh!' Tom was making reference to the snow earlier in the week.

Smurve had served Tom, pulled a pint for himself and wondered what I was going for.

'Let's show willing and have a Humbug mate please.' I confirmed. Tom in the meantime had stoked his pipe up.

Beryl and Ian were the next customers in. They were professional people living in Wye and came to the pub on most bank holidays. They weren't major users, as they had difficulties in getting baby sitters and a vehicle big enough to carry everyone at once. They had both been in previous relationships and had a large tribe of children. There were six in all, five from their previous partners, and Claire the youngest, their own child. Bank holidays were easier because parents in law normally came to visit and solved the logistics issue. Ian was a real ale enthusiast and a pipe man like Tom. He intended trying all the ales before leaving. Beryl had agreed to drive and her father had also drawn the short straw. Today was very special for Ian. Christmas Eve, great real ales, all the family and no driving – it was time to celebrate! He pulled out his 'ceremonial' Sherlock

Holmes style of pipe. The pipe had a massive bowl which he was packing with Hearts of Oak tobacco. Pungent aromatic smoke was soon being wafted about. He started his mission with a pint of Wadworths 6X – what more could a man ask for. Beryl in the meantime had taken crisps and drinks outside to the kids in the garden. The Herbie tree was in demand again from the children. Our two girls went out to join in the fun with Ian and Beryl's children. I have to say it was a lovely relaxed and cosy atmosphere in the bar. Nice and easygoing with good friendly people. I bought the next round of beer for everyone as it was unlikely Beryl and Ian would be with us the following morning. Both Tom and Ian were really enjoying their pipes as the AK gang joined us in their entirety. Bob, Sal, Christina, Jack and Mrs. Rose was not far behind. Everyone was full of optimism and cheer. The bright winter sunshine and the imminence of Christmas probably had a lot to do with it. The restaurant area was filling up rapidly and keeping Sara and the girls in the kitchen 'on their toes'.

Deidre had come in to help out and just as well. Our steak meals were in high demand. Luckily I had increased our steak order just on the off chance. My foresight had paid off handsomely on this occasion.

Back in the bar, the pace was increasing for Smurve and me. Ian and Tom continued to enjoy their pipe-smoking habits together. They both had settled in for a full session and were 'sinking' their beers fast and furiously.

I couldn't help but notice through the window the children were all playing quite happily in the garden. I remarked to Ian and Beryl that it was good to see all the children getting on so well. In particular I thought bringing up the black gorilla fancy dress suit was a particularly good move.

'What the hell are you on about' Ian asked

'You're eldest out there, running around in the black fur monkey suit' I replied.

'We haven't got a monkey suit!' Ian nonchalantly remarked after taking another drink on his beer and followed up with a further draw on his pipe.

'It looks like it too me. It's monkey business or something!' Tom remarked whilst looking out the window.

Ian was still not in the slightest bit perturbed.

Smurve remarked 'He's at it again!' as the fur clad 'thing' ran by the window.

The penny finally dropped after seeing Amanda and Kate chasing closely behind.

Someone had left the gate open and Roscoe decided he was going to join in the fun as well. After all it was Christmas. His bad, over-sexed habit had reared its head again! He had obviously taken a real romantic fancy to Ian and Beryl's eldest son, Jonathan. No matter how Jonathan tried to avoid Roscoe, he was having none of it!

'Bloody hell, it's Roscoe!' I panicked and flew out of the bar to the assistance of poor Jonathan. I pulled Roscoe off and took him back to the rear garden, chastising him all the way. Luckily, Jonathan who was coming sixteen saw the funny-side of the episode. Ian for his part came out to see if there was any damage. Having had a couple of drinks already, he could hardly contain himself.

'Monkeys and Gorillas!' Whatever next as he fell about laughing. Jonathan followed suit as did the rest of the children.

We returned to the bar and I got Amanda to come in and get more drinks, crisps and snacks for them all.

What a morning! The session finished later than normal due to the extended drinking hour extension. We were all relieved to close up after the last customers left and put our feet up and relax. We were only halfway through our first exhausting Christmas Eve at the pub. As per the norm, we were ready for the fray by 7.00pm. All the staff members were in and ready for action. We were fully booked in the restaurant for the night. Sue, Deidre and Molly had prepared themselves for a run on steak meals, following on from the earlier lunchtime session.

The evening extension was most poignant as I had been approached to allow a troupe of local carol singers with keyboard accompaniment to perform in the pub before leaving to attend midnight mass at Hastingleigh Church with James Hume. The extra extension meant the carol singers and churchgoers could be accommodated and also still have time for a night cap afterwards if they so desired. Regardless of our customer's intentions, we would be fully committed to constantly trading throughout.

I agreed to the carol singers from 10.00pm onwards. It was their intention to go around a selection of pubs in the area. The Dew Drop Inn would be the last to be visited as we were the nearest to

Hastingleigh church and the agreed timing of the troupe's appearance.
The evening trade started where the lunchtime left off. Locals and regulars were all back in, having a good time to boot. There was standing room only and not much of that either.
It was a more relaxed atmosphere than normal and there appeared to be genuine 'goodwill' to all men. There was a very 'Christmassy' feel to the whole evening.
The carol singers arrived slightly earlier than planned and set themselves up for their performance. Due to the lack of space in the bar, the choir had to site themselves in the entrance porch. With the door wedged open, the sound travelled through into the bar area and restaurant. It added a nice touch to the last trading session before Christmas Day and was very well accepted by all the customers. I believe the troupe's charitable collection benefited considerably, making their visit very worthwhile.
The troupe finished their performance. I offered them all a drink on the house which was very gratefully accepted. Smurve and I poured their requested drinks and served them to the troupe members. They drank up pretty promptly as they were expected to be at the Church shortly afterwards. Shortly after the troupe left I rang the bell and announced the imminent start of Midnight Mass for those interested. There weren't that many takers, so the session continued unabated. On the stroke of midnight I range the bell again making everyone aware it was Christmas Day. Most customers wished each other Happy Christmas, continuing the friendly ambience throughout.
Customers started to leave shortly after midnight. We all wished each other well as they left. The kitchen closedown had been completed some time earlier. The girls were all in the bar enjoying themselves and 'unwinding' after their earlier efforts. On my instructions Smurve ensured their glasses were kept full. They deserved their reward!
The last customers finally left at 1.20am. Smurve, Sue and I were left in the bar. We were pretty exhausted but not mentally tired. Sue decided to go upstairs and get ready for bed. Smurve and I celebrated Christmas with a couple of Johnny Walker Black Label whiskies and then called it a night.
I locked up after Smurve left, but not before going out to the car to bring in the massive Scalectrix box set and the jewellery gifts for my 'girls'. I left the girls box in the entrance porch purposely because I

had to 'let Santa in and deliver' as our chimney was way too small to accommodate such a large box! I left an empty sherry glass, a plate with a piece of mince pie on it and a couple of carrots alongside the box with a 'Thank you' note from Santa and Rudolph.
I turned the lights out and went up to bed.
We were greeted on Christmas morning in our bedroom, shortly after 7.00am with 'Mum, Dad he's been!' An overly excited Kate, the youngest daughter had obviously got up and been downstairs, presumably to go through the daily 'Roscoe' routine we had discovered earlier. This time however, Roscoe came in second place! She had been into the entrance porch and found the enormous parcel that Santa had left the girls, the remains of his mince pie and his reindeers' carrots. Santa had even drunk all the sherry left out for him. Trying to absorb all this information from an over-excited seven year old, having had barely four hours sleep was exceedingly difficult. Having heard the commotion, Amanda came into our room to hear the repeated rendition from her younger sister of Santa's earlier visit.
In my bleary stupor, I confessed to hearing the knock at the door at 2.00am. Santa had to apologise for disturbing me, but felt it necessary because the chimney was far too small to take the box with him down into the fireplace below. I agreed and took the big box in from him, gave him his drink and mince pie then fed the reindeers. They all left shortly afterwards.
'Why not go downstairs and see what he's brought you. You are really lucky!' I suggested in the hope it might gain Sue and me an extra hour or so of sleep.
No such luck! Sue had promised both girls a Scalectrix set for Christmas earlier. It had clearly made their day. Both girls had returned to our bedroom pleading for me to get up and set the car racing set up.
'No rest for the wicked. I shouldn't have been so bad in my previous life!' I muttered to Sue as I slowly dragged myself out of bed. Sue didn't answer or respond; she was oblivious to my moaning and was back with the fairies!
I went downstairs and into the kitchen, put the kettle on and made two mugs ready for tea. The girls in the meantime had manhandled the big box between them into the restaurant. Realistically, as the restaurant was not in use that day it was the only place to set up the

racetrack. We moved the tables and chairs back to the walls to make space for the layout.

The tea was made and I took a mug up to Sue with the jewellery gifts I had bought the day earlier. She finally woke up and I wished her Happy Christmas again, gave her the mug of tea and her gifts. I left to go back downstairs as there was a more pressing track to be constructed.

The box had been opened and sections of track were being laid out by the girls. I suggested a nice figure of eight layout. We all agreed and started clipping the components together. It was a lot bigger than I expected, it was just as well we had plenty of room to play with. Finally after about three quarters of an hour the track was complete. I connected the controllers and transformer and we were ready for the first run. The two Ferrari racing cars were put on the track in their respective grooves. Amanda was to drive the blue car, Kate the red one. I was official starter and they were away first time. Sue had managed to pull herself out of bed and came downstairs to watch the proceedings. She came over and sat on my lap, gave me a sensuous kiss, told me what a bad boy I was and went on to thank me, whilst showing me her new bracelet on her wrist! I told her the charms were from the girls. For their part they were only interested in the race in hand.

Time was getting on and despite all the fun the girls were having I had a bar to open in less than three hours. I got up and set about the bar preparation. Despite such a busy evening before I was surprised that the cleaning operations were completed reasonably quickly. Bottling up was not quite so simple. Our shelves were pretty empty of bottle stock. The 'empties' had been piled up in the rear store. They had to be sorted, crated up and stacked outside for collection later. Not the most glamorous or amusing job for Christmas morning but it had to be done. Only then could new bottles be shelf stacked in the bar back fittings. In the cellar the stockholdings of all the beers needed checking. After the busy sessions I was not surprised to find some of the kegs were running low. Three kegs needed to be changed and new reserves taken in to the cellar, much to Roscoe's delight. The real ales had similarly taken a 'hammering'. Reserve stock had been prepared previously so a simple spear slide down was required. Two of the spirit optics needed re-stocking and I was done. The final hoovering through and the toilet floor areas mopped completed the cleaning. The fires could be lit and we were pretty well ready for action. Smurve turned up as arranged and lit the fires for me. We were in fact well ahead of time and that gave us the opportunity to have breakfast together and a bit of Formula One practice!

We enjoyed a full English breakfast each, washed down with plenty of fresh coffee. Sue had suggested we use up some sausage rolls and mince pies in the bar with the normal roast potatoes. I agreed and said not to bother with the normal sausages and cheese.

I left Smurve being given a hard time on the track by our girls and went up for a swift shower. Sue had already 'dolled' herself up whilst I was preparing the bar.

On the stroke of twelve we opened the doors. I was not entirely sure how many people we could expect as it was Christmas morning. People may well have had more important things on their mind rather than going to the pub.

It goes to show in this game, you never can be sure.

Chris, his wife and full family were first in. There were seven of them and had made arrangements to meet Phil and Ed, their nephews from over the road. Colin and Suzanne weren't far behind with Colin's two sons and wives from his previous marriage.

Compliments of the season were offered all around; kisses under the mistletoe were rife whilst Smurve and I were responding to the rising tide of business. The first free drink went down well again with the customers.

Sue came out to the bar with the roast potatoes and trays of sausage rolls and mince pies.

The AK Gang in their entirety arrived along with the full Rose clan. It really was nice to have all our regulars together. The friendly atmosphere was building all the time. Terry and Molly came across with their children. Mark and Jody were immediately met by Amanda and Kate and ushered in to the restaurant for battle on the track to commence.

Tom was on top form.

'Ere boy! What's this I hear? Santa came and couldn't down your chimney, eh?' Tom had obviously seen the girls earlier that morning and spilt the beans on my earlier action.

'Yeah, had to open the door and let 'im in! It must have been about two!' I replied

'Happy Christmas mate!' he responded and toasting me with his pot.
'Cheers Tom!'

Shortly after 12.30 we had a visit from Revd James Hume. He had come in with his son and had not long finished the normal family morning Eucharist. It had overrun a little that day being Christmas Day.

'Good morning James, Happy Christmas. Just finished have you? What can I get you?' I asked.

'Happy Christmas to you too old chap. What do you recommend? I do like a good beer.' he went on.

This made me feel a little uneasy,

His son saved the day.

'Two pints of Humbug please.' he asked

James Hume was a secret real ale fan and tippler unbeknown to me. I duly pulled them two pints and explained they were on the house. They both appreciated the gesture and set about their beers.

'Mmm.....delicious!' the vicar said whilst smacking his lips.

'I'm finished for the day. It's a special day and I'm up for it!' he continued.

Smurve overheard the vicar's comments and whispered in my ear.

'Can a vicar say and do that?'

I replied 'I s'pose so. They can get just as pissed as the rest of us. It is a celebration day!'

Smurve chuckled to himself.

'Were your girls happy with what Santa brought them?' James asked after which he took another gulp of his beer.

'You can see for yourself later on James.' I replied.

His son had finished his beer and ordered a repeat round, offering a £10 note to pay this time. I pulled up another couple of pints and returned the change. The vicar and his son didn't wait long to attack the next round.

I turned to Smurve and offered him a pint. He nodded and whilst I had the time pulled up his pint and an Old Thumper for me.

The whole session was moving along very nicely. Sue was passing through the bar with sausage rolls and mince pies to ensure everyone had one at least. She knew James Hume through the school. She found her way over too him and offered them the food. They helped themselves saying how nice it was and they were starving.

Starving and thirsty – hard old work being a vicar I concluded.

Jim came to the bar for the AK Gang refill. As I was pouring their mild Jim caught me completely unawares.

'Do you know old chap, since the two of you have taken over the old place it's never been so alive. Thanks for everything!' He said in all sincerity.
'Well that's great to hear! Thanks for that old Man!' I was quite touched at his remark.
Jim paid for the round and passed the refills around.
Time was moving on. It was just before 2.30 and the bar was thinning out. Most of the women had left, presumably to complete their own Christmas lunch preparations.
The men folk remaining were all enjoying themselves immensely, the vicar in particular.
Smurve had advised me that he had seen me pull the Old Thumper for myself and concluded that it was probably 'the beer' to be drinking. I wouldn't argue with that!
James and his son absolutely loved their first experience of the Old Thumper. So much so they were ready to start on their second pint. I pulled it for them and took the payment.
'You need to be careful of drinking and driving with that James!' I pointed out.
The vicar gave me a somewhat candid stare. As if a vicar would do such a thing is how I read it!
'Go on through to the restaurant and see what Santa brought the girls?' I instructed
He got up and went through to the restaurant and wasn't seen for a little while.
His son was all the more confused.
'We're not driving you know. My wife is coming to pick us up at 3.00.' he explained.
'I know old mate. I'm having a bit of a laugh as you will see! Trust me – enjoy your beer!' I left him for about 15 minutes, the time it took to finish his pint.
'Phil you have the same again?' I asked
'Yes please. Best have one for the old man as well!'
I pulled the two beers and put them on the bar. He paid for them. I asked him to wait a second and popped out of the bar into the restaurant.
What a sight to see!
James was on the floor with the four children. He was trying to master the blue Ferrari with a bit of assistance from Amanda. He was

struggling a little; perhaps the quantity of Old Thumper and Humbug had something to do with it?
I quickly went back to the bar and told his son to take the beers into the restaurant. I rushed back through to the restaurant again, picking up a polythene bag from the kitchen.
I waited for James's son to appear and put down the recharged glasses of Old Thumper. The vicar was having a great time but was no match for any of the children. I made my move.
'Excuse me sir! Have you had a drink in the last 20 minutes?' addressing the vicar.
He stopped for a second and looked up at me.
'Could I ask you to blow into this bag please? One long slow blow' I continued holding out the polythene bag.
His son just burst out laughing. The children all followed suit. Poor old James Hume had been caught fair and square.
I had the last word.
'Drinking and Driving Scalectrix is very much frowned on in this pub!'
He held his hands up
'It's a fair cop officer! I'm guilty as charged'
We all had a laugh and James got stuck in to his Old Thumper pint.
I went back to the bar and rang the bell for last orders.
A lot of customers had taken the hint, thanked us for a good time and left for their Christmas Lunch and The Queen at 3.00.
The last customers to leave were Tom, Terry and his children, the vicar and his son. As pre-arranged the vicar's daughter-in-law collected the pair to return them to the vicarage. Everyone who attended seemed to have had a good time.
Smurve was in no rush to getaway. We tidied up and did the closedown procedures as quickly as possible. Our Christmas could finally begin.
It started with our own Christmas grand prix!

EPILOGUE

All in all we had been in residence and owners of The Dew Drop Inn for nearly our first year. Newcomers can find it notoriously difficult to be accepted in to the country scene. We appeared to have been very well accepted, fitting in within the small country community of Bodsham Green. It hadn't been easy and there were moments when we both felt like walking away. However, there had been special moments that had made it all very worthwhile. The friendship shown to us by the local residents of our hamlet will be remembered for many a year after leaving.

We had been extremely lucky to find good staff to help out and play their parts in the overall success of the business. Our sincere thanks go out to all of them.

Our customers active support was also very much appreciated. They provided the income and very life blood for our country pub existence. Thank you to everyone.

Sadly, it appears the days of the traditional country pub are numbered. High running costs, excessive taxes and demands with diminishing returns are strangling the life out of the trade. It is a tradition that will be sadly missed when it is gone.

We were both appreciative of being able to 'live the dream' before the opportunity disappeared.

Printed in Dunstable, United Kingdom